More Than Singing

Discovering Music in Preschool and Kindergarten

by
Sally Moomaw

Redleaf Press

Photography by David C. Baxter, University of Cincinnati

Published by: Redleaf Press
a division of Resources for Child Caring
450 N. Syndicate, Suite 5
St. Paul, MN 55104

Library of Congress Cataloging-in-Publication Data

Moomaw, Sally.
More than singing : discovering music in preschool and kindergarten / by Sally Moomaw.
p. cm.
Includes bibliographical references (p.).
ISBN 1-884834-34-5 (alk. paper)
1. School music--Instruction and study--Activity programs. 2. Nursery schools--Music. I. Title.
MT10.M6676 1997
372.87'044--dc21 97-19869
CIP
MN

For Charlie

Acknowledgments

My first thanks must go to my family. My husband performed the tedious and, to me, complex task of entering all the music into the computer. He also arranged songs for the recording; performed the recorder, bassoon, and percussion parts; constantly mediated between the computer and me; and kept me afloat throughout the project. Thanks, Charlie. I would also like to thank my son Peter for performing guitar on the recording and contributing several songs to the book, and my son Jeff for entertaining us with his gymnastics and providing some needed balance to our lives.

I am indebted to my colleague and good friend Brenda Hieronymus for sharing her teaching ideas, for helping to organize children for the photographs, for her constant inspiration as an early childhood teacher, and especially for lending her lovely singing voice to the recording.

David C. Baxter of PhotoGraphic Services, University of Cincinnati, who did all of the photographic work for the book, deserves special thanks. His patience, good humor, and artistic suggestions were greatly appreciated.

I also wish to thank the following people who contributed to the recording: Terry Roberston, vocals; Claire Dunnington, who announced the activity numbers; and John Burgess, Studio Director and Recording Engineer at WGUC-FM, Cincinnati. The music was recorded in the Corbett Recording Studio at WGUC.

Some of the instruments used in the activities are modeled after instruments made by the Percussion Group, Ensemble-in-Residence at the University of Cincinnati College-Conservatory of Music. I appreciate the willingness of Professor Allen Otte to share his time and ideas.

I thank my colleagues at the Arlitt Child and Family Research and Education Center, University of Cincinnati, for their enthusiasm and support. Facilities, equipment, and materials from the center were used in some of the photographs in the book.

Many individuals contributed words from their languages to use in activities in this book. I would like to thank Khemara Dinh (Cambodian), Ting Chen (Chinese), Rinna Sanchez (Filipino), Laura Samuels (Hebrew), Srinivas Medicherla (Hindi), Sony and Maya Miarsono (Indonesian), Eriko Kobayashi and Masayo Nakamura (Japanese), Susan Tsai (Korean), Guy W. Jones (Lakota), Amy Ploysangam (Thai), and Shoaib Usman (Urdu).

Thanks are also due to Jon and Sally Kamholtz for their feedback on thorny grammatical issues.

A special thanks goes to the children who participated in the photo sessions: Samudra, Elijah, Kate, Alice, Allison, Angki, Anne, Annie, Ayan, Ayanna, Charles, David, Emily, Katie, Loren, Lori, Mengyue, Simone, Sumedha, Tiffany, and Wesley.

Finally, I would like to thank my editor at Redleaf Press, Mary Steiner Whelan, for her encouragement, help, and enthusiasm.

Sally Moomaw
April, 1997

Contents

Preface

Music in some form, whether it be finger plays, simple songs, or the occasional use of rhythm sticks, is a part of most early childhood programs. However, many teachers of young children do not realize the wealth of musical experiences they can plan, even though they may not be trained musicians. *More Than Singing* fills that gap in early childhood curriculum. Teachers will find ideas for setting up music areas in their classrooms where children can explore concepts of sound and create their own music. Teachers will learn how to make resonant, inexpensive instruments and utilize instruments in many different ways. They will gain knowledge about how to select songs and rhythm activities and coordinate them with whole-language materials. They will also find new suggestions for movement activities and ideas for incorporating music throughout the day.

More Than Singing contains over a hundred music activities. An introductory chapter is followed by chapters on songs, rhythm, instruments, music centers, movement, music throughout the day, and group times. Chapters 2 through 8 each contain two sections: answers to questions that teachers frequently ask and activities that help children construct knowledge about sound and create music. Photographs of instruments and whole-language extensions accompany guidelines on how to construct the materials. Thus, teachers can easily duplicate the suggested activities. The cassette tape that accompanies this book contains all of the songs and rhythms described in the activities. This enables those who do not read music to hear all of the musical examples.

Throughout this book, reference is made to teachers and their role in guiding young children in the discovery of music and the construction of musical concepts. The term *teachers* is meant to be inclusive. All those who work with young children are teachers, whether they are parents, child care workers, or classroom aides. This book is designed to meet the needs of the wide spectrum of people who care for and nurture young children.

Music is an integral part of young children's lives and should also be an integrated part of early childhood programs. *More Than Singing* gives ideas for coordinating music with literature, math activities, and thematic units. Thus, music becomes another tool for enhancing the overall curriculum. Suggestions for integrated curriculum activities accompany the activities in chapters 2 through 6. Chapter 7 provides information on ways to incorporate music throughout the day, introduce music in diverse areas of the classroom, and utilize music as a transition tool.

Teachers often have questions about planning and implementing group music experiences. Chapter 8 explains how to incorporate many aspects of music into group time plans and coordinate them with other circle time activities. Transitions to and from group time activities as well as pacing the group are discussed. Sample lesson plans are included to serve as guidelines for teachers as they incorporate their own ideas into group time experiences.

Music is an excellent tool for exploring multicultural dimensions in curriculum. Multicultural curriculum suggestions in this book include ideas for introducing various languages into songs and rhythm activities (activities 2.6, 2.12, and 3.3); exploring instruments from many cultures (activities 5.5, 5.6, 5.8, 5.12, and 5.13); and a multicultural listening guide with scaffolding suggestions for teachers as they introduce children to recorded music from diverse cultures (activity 7.16). At the back of the book there is a list containing the publication information for the specific books and recordings mentioned in the activities.

Many early childhood classrooms include children with disabilities. Like typically developing children, they often respond enthusiastically to music activities. Suggestions for modifying music activities for inclusion children appear in the "Teachers' Questions" sections of chapters 2, 4, and 6. Activities 2.17 and 7.4 are designed specifically for inclusion children.

Music for young children spans cultural, socioeconomic, and ability differences. Teachers, child care workers, and parents can all participate in the enrichment that music, in its many forms, brings to the lives of children. May this book serve as a guide in those endeavors.

CHAPTER

The Music-Rich Classroom

Open the door to the classroom and listen:

On one side of the room, children hear a recording of quiet music played on Native American flute, piano, and cello. They draw, paint, write, and create collages as they listen.

In the classroom's music area, a child compares the sounds made by two sizes of triangles.

Across the room, three children sing a song together as they point to the words on a chart and add one another's names to the text.

▲ ▲ ▲

Music is important in the lives of children. They sing as they play. They grow silent and intent when they hear unusual sounds. They become quiet and relaxed when they listen to soothing sounds. They move their bodies in concert with the music they hear. Music is central to the human experience of children. In a music-rich classroom, it permeates the environment.

Why is music so meaningful to children? Why is it such an important part of the early childhood curriculum?

- ▲ Music provides ***emotional release***. Children use songs and rhythms as an outlet to express and work through emotions and to communicate their thoughts and feelings.
- ▲ Music encourages ***cultural sharing***. Music stimulates cultural awareness as children listen to recordings and explore instruments from around the world.
- ▲ Music increases ***physical knowledge***. Through experimenting with how sound is created (whether it is producing sounds with their voices or with instruments), children form concepts about the nature of sound and music. They gain an awareness of how their actions alter sound.

- ▲ Music heightens ***listening skills***. Children develop more refined listening skills through music experiences. They must listen carefully to learn a tune or rhythm. Children begin to focus on individual aspects of music as they also hear the whole.
- ▲ Music aids ***cognitive development***. Neurological research indicates that exposure to music heightens children's cognitive development and helps them develop complex reasoning skills.[1]
- ▲ Music experiences foster ***appreciation***. Musical development is also an outcome for children in a music-rich environment. Children gain a feel for rhythm and the beat in music. They learn to stay together as they sing and play instruments, and they begin to attend to particular aspects of music such as tempo, dynamics, and pitch.
- ▲ Music assists in ***motor development***. Music helps children develop motor skills and body awareness. Movements that require one side of the body to move independently of the other encourage children's lateral development. Other movements reinforce awareness of body parts. Finally, moving in many different ways to a variety of music helps children develop coordination and encourages imagination.
- ▲ Music is a tool for ***scaffolding***. Music can provide a bridge to learning for children who experience language, physical, mental, or emotional barriers.
- ▲ Music increases ***self-esteem***. Music also fosters a positive self-image since every child can feel successful in music activities. Many songs focus on children themselves and encourage their ideas.

Music and the Young Child

Children construct musical knowledge as they explore, by concrete means, the many different aspects of sound and music. The children must be active participants in the music-making process. Only by actually producing sounds with a variety of materials, or through active involvement with music, do children come to a real understanding of what makes sound and music. Singing, clapping, moving to music, making up songs, and playing instruments are some of the many ways children can experience music.

In order to plan appropriate music activities, teachers must understand the developmental stages of children and how those stages relate to music. Although individual differences in the rate of development vary widely, the sequence of development follows a particular pattern. The table on the following pages contains behavioral characteristics for each stage of development along with their effect on children's perception of music. The material is based on the theories of Piaget, Erikson, and on the writings of Todd and Heffernan.[2]

Relationship of Developmental Characteristics of Children to Music

Age	Behavioral Characteristics	Music Experiences
Newborns to 1 Month	develop trust versus mistrust in environment	are soothed by quiet singing and rocking, which help them formulate trust are frightened by scary sounds, which can lead to mistrust
	respond to stimuli reflexively by moving entire body	are attuned to sound stimuli react to sound by moving entire body
1 to 4 Months	make first differentiations change from hearing to listening turn head toward stimulus follow moving objects with eyes	turn head in direction of sound follow sound of moving object if it is readily visible
4 to 8 Months	are interested in cause-and-effect relationships engage in purposeful activity reproduce interesting events develop eye-hand coordination	hit suspended bells again and again to reproduce the sound
8 to 12 Months	coordinate two schemata anticipate events, exhibit intention know that objects have stable functions imitate actions	strike drum or xylophone with a mallet clap hands to music hit instruments to produce a sound understand purpose of instrument
12 to 18 Months	invent new actions use trial and error to solve problems	experiment by hitting instruments in different ways with different objects

Age	Behavioral Characteristics	Music Experiences
18 to 24 Months	create new actions through prior thought	continue music activities after adult stops
	imitate actions after person leaves	
2 Years	step in place pat run	enjoy action songs and moving to music
	show increased language development	can learn short, simple songs
	have short attention spans attend to spoken words a few at a time	can focus on activities with short, simple directions
	develop autonomy are very curious	seek out opportunities to experiment with instruments and sound
3 Years	jump, run, and walk to music	respond to tempo and mood in music with particular movements
	have more self-control	can wait briefly for a turn
	have longer attention spans show increased vocabulary	can sing somewhat longer songs and participate in small group experiences
	compare two objects	experiment with sound comparisons
	participate in planning	suggest words for songs or additional activities
	are developing initiative	need choices along with opportunities to try out their own ideas
4 Years	have better motor control	may begin skipping
	are interested in rules	enjoy noncompetitive games and songs with rules
	plan ahead with adults	can make suggestions for music activities
	like to imagine	add words to songs create songs on instruments create dramatic movements
5 and 6 Years	have increased motor control	able to sit longer for music experiences
	are very conscious of rules	enjoy songs and dances with rules recognize and reproduce specific rhythm patterns

Music and the Early Childhood Teacher

The early childhood teacher plays a crucial role in planning and sharing music experiences with young children. Unfortunately, some teachers feel inadequate in the area of music. Many erroneously believe that they need special talent or training in order to explore music with young children.

Music is for everyone. All teachers can plan and implement music activities with children, just as they facilitate art experiences without being artists, promote science exploration without being scientists, and encourage gross-motor activities without being athletes.

Children are not music critics. They respond enthusiastically to teachers who are willing to sing with them, even if the teachers do not regard themselves as musicians. In addition to leading children in group music experiences and modeling the pleasure of creating music, teachers play a key role in facilitating children's explorations of sound and music. Although a well-planned music environment entices children to experiment, it is the teacher who guides children's construction of musical knowledge by stimulating their thinking and helping them refine their observations.

Music and the Early Childhood Classroom

The music environment unfolds at three levels:

1. The music area of the classroom
2. Group time experiences that incorporate music
3. Throughout the entire classroom, both through spontaneous interjection of music and by planned spin-offs into other areas of the curriculum

The music center is an area of the classroom where children can explore sound and create music. Although the area is a permanent part of the classroom, teachers can regularly change the instruments or other materials to reflect long-range goals, the overall classroom curriculum, and input from the children. (You'll find information about setting up music centers and planning activities for them in chapter 5.)

Music making is often a shared group experience. Orchestras, bands, and choruses all involve groups of musicians combining to produce music. Children also enjoy the experience of the communal creation of music, and group times provide this opportunity. Through singing, exploring rhythms, playing instruments, and creating movements, children can share musical experiences. (You'll find ideas for activities in all of these areas in chapters 2,

3, 4, and 6, respectively. You'll find ideas for putting music activities together into cohesive group times in chapter 8.)

Music opportunities abound throughout the day, so teachers need not relegate music to just one portion of the classroom schedule. Children sing spontaneously as they play, and they appreciate hearing recorded music as part of their environment. They respond positively to interjections of singing into other areas of the curriculum as well as songs to help with transitions. (You'll find ideas for incorporating music throughout the day in chapter 7.)

Goals

What, then, should be the goals of music experiences with young children? Children should:

- Have many opportunities to explore music through singing, playing instruments, and creating body movements
- Gain increased understanding of what affects sound
- Have opportunities to expand their listening skills
- Develop increased enjoyment and appreciation of music
- Have opportunities to hear and explore the music of other cultures
- Explore their own creativity in music
- Have opportunities to express emotions through music
- Develop increased awareness of body image and self-identity
- Have experiences that reflect their developmental needs
- Have opportunities for group participation in music making

Teachers can achieve these broad goals by providing a wide variety of musical experiences and allowing for as much input from children as possible. Teachers need to provide for both individual experimentation and group participation. The music curriculum should encompass a broad spectrum of music activities, and the environment should encourage frequent and autonomous exploration of sound and the process of music making. Only then can children maximize their potentials as imitators, experimenters, creators, and participants in the realm of music.

Endnotes

1. Information about research by Frances H. Rauscher and Gordon L. Shaw regarding the effect of music on cognition in preschool children is available from the Center for the Neurobiology of Learning and Memory, University of California, Irvine, CA 92717.
2. Barry J. Wadsworth, *Piaget's Theory of Cognitive and Affective Development*, 4th ed. (White Plains, NY: Longman, 1989).
   Erik K. Erikson, *Childhood and Society,* 2nd ed. (New York: Norton, 1963).
   Vivian Edmiston Todd and Helen Heffernan, *The Years before School,* 2nd ed. (New York: Macmillan, 1970).

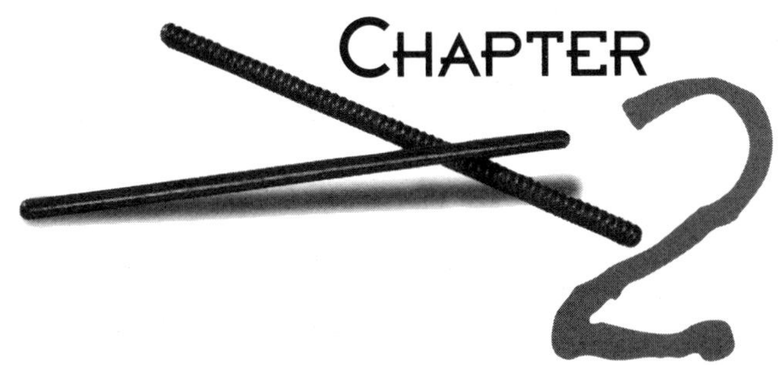

Songs

Three-year-old Carina made a microphone with snap blocks and began to sing a song about her mother.

A second child, Ren-Jye, also made a microphone and began singing in his own language.

Soon a third child with her own microphone joined the group, and all three children began dancing as they sang.

▲ ▲ ▲

Songs are central to the musical experiences of young children. Most children sing spontaneously from an early age whether or not they are ever formally taught a song. Since singing is an important means of expression for young children, teachers should include songs as a daily part of their curriculum.

What makes a good song for young children? Teachers quickly discover that not every song works with every group. Teachers must choose carefully when deciding on songs, just as careful attention must be given to selecting books for the classroom. Soon they develop a repertoire of songs for various times of the year or thematic topics, just as they have particular books that are mainstays.

Teachers' Questions

What criteria should teachers consider when selecting songs?

Teachers should consider:

- ▲ The length of the song
- ▲ The repetitiveness of the melody and words
- ▲ The content or subject matter of the song

- ▲ The range of the song
- ▲ How well the song coordinates with the rest of the curriculum

How long should the song be?

The length of the song depends on the age of the children. A song that is too long and complex will not hold children's attention, and they may quickly lose interest in one that is too short and simple.

Toddlers need very short, simple songs. Since appropriate songs for toddlers are about one line in length, they are sometimes called *sentence songs*.

Three year olds are ready for slightly longer songs. Although they may still enjoy some very short songs, in general they prefer slightly longer and more complex songs. Four-line songs are typical.

Four- and five-year-old children enjoy longer and more complicated songs. Since the dynamics of each group of children is different, the teacher must assess what level of song is appropriate for that group. In general, however, older preschool and kindergarten children enjoy the challenge of six- to eight-line songs or songs with more than one verse.

Each activity in this chapter indicates the age level for which it is most appropriate.

Why is the repetition of words and melody important?

Young children love repetition, and songs with repetitive words and melody are easier for them to sing and to remember. Children gravitate toward predictable books for the same reason. In many of the songs in this book, both the melody and words repeat. The song "Autumn Leaves" (activity 2.5) is a good example.

What constitutes good content in a song for young children?

The subject matter should be relevant to the lives of young children. Songs about children, families, animals, transportation, weather, and community workers are appropriate because these are topics familiar to young children. For example, the song "Thunder" (activity 2.10), readily appeals to many young children because they have experienced thunderstorms and are struggling to understand them.

Songs that encourage children to express their feelings or use their imaginations are also important. A song like "Clouds" (activity 2.8) stimulates young imaginations. The words were composed by a three year old as he watched the sky. Each child can add something different to the song.

What topics should teachers avoid?

Some songs commonly taught to preschool children are inappropriate for their stage of development or deal with subject matter that is completely foreign to the young child. Many nursery rhymes fit this category. For example, "Hey Diddle Diddle," a rhyme or song many adults remember from childhood, is confusing to young preschoolers. Since they are still trying to separate reality from fantasy, young preschool children typically do not appreciate the humor of the cow jumping over the moon. After hearing this song, one three year old asked for the moon to be brought down so that he could jump over it too. Piaget describes the magical thinking of the preoperational child and reminds us that children at this stage believe the moon is following them. When teachers select songs such as "Hey Diddle Diddle," they reinforce prelogical thinking in young children. Songs that reflect the real-life experiences of children are a better choice.

Frightening songs may surface around Halloween. Songs about witches and goblins often scare young children who may believe that people dressed up in costumes have actually turned into the creatures they are pretending to be. A song that emphasizes the pretend nature of Halloween, such as "No Witches" (activity 2.16), can be helpful in countering these fears.

Avoid songs that reinforce stereotypes. Unfortunately, such songs still abound. A song in a kindergarten music book adopted by many school systems says, in part: "Playing Indian is such fun . . . Hi-yah! Hi-yah! Hi!" "Did you ever see a Crow paddling a canoe?" and "Let's pretend we're Iroquois, shooting with our bows." Songs such as this perpetuate inaccurate and stereotypical images of Native Americans and objectify and degrade them as a people. For this reason, Native American educational organizations such as Oyate[1] urge teachers to stop having children sing songs like "10 Little Indians." Teachers can ask themselves if they would feel comfortable putting any other race into such a song.

Watch for gender bias in songs you teach, just as you would with children's literature. For example, be sure that songs about doctors and firefighters use feminine as well as masculine pronouns, while songs about nurses and cooks portray boys as well as girls. Watch for songs that depict boys as strong and courageous, while girls are described as pretty.

How high or low should the song go?

Young children have a narrow range to their voices. Although we often think of young children as having very high singing voices, this is true of older elementary school children, not preschool and kindergarten children. Their voices tend to be much lower. When young children try to sing songs that are too high or too low, they are forced to sing out of tune or strain their voices. Teachers of three year olds should select songs that lie primarily between middle C and five to six notes above it. Four- to five-year-old children are usually comfortable singing between middle C and the C eight notes above it. Many songs for young children lie in this range.

Young children can most easily sing songs that move by step or have small skips between the notes. Songs with large skips are more difficult for them to sing.

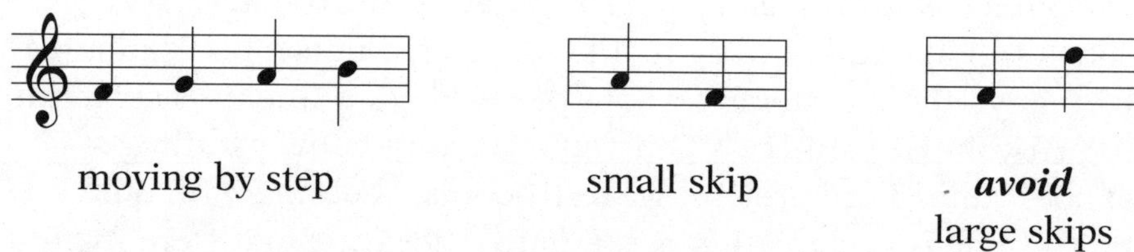

Why should teachers coordinate songs with the overall curriculum?

Songs take on added meaning when teachers coordinate them with the rest of the curriculum. Songs can also reinforce learning in other curriculum areas. For example, if the class has taken a trip to the zoo or is planning one, songs about zoo animals would be of added interest to the children and might help them remember the names or characteristics of the animals. If the class has been experimenting with planting seeds, then songs about plants and growing would help reinforce those concepts. While not every song needs to correlate with the rest of the curriculum, it is good planning to include many that do.

What is the best way to teach a song?

Children learn songs best when the teacher sings the entire song several times and repeats it over a period of several days. When teachers break up songs into individual lines in order to teach them, young children quickly lose continuity, meaning, and interest. Therefore, it is best to sing the entire song and let children participate whenever they feel ready. At first, children may wish to join in on certain parts of a song while the teacher sings the entire song.

Although children can also learn songs from listening to recordings, they seem to learn best and participate most fully when they can follow a live singer. Often the performer on recordings sings too fast for young children or has a voice that lies in a different range from theirs. When teachers sing with children, they can vary the speed of the song and adjust the range to fit their own groups. For this reason, while teachers may wish to use recordings to teach themselves songs, they are encouraged to actually sing the songs when teaching them to children.

Remember, children are not music critics. They are delighted to sing along with their teacher even if the teacher does not consider herself much of a singer.

How can teachers find songs on particular topics?

Look for song books at the library, and use the criteria listed earlier in this chapter to evaluate each song. Consult other teachers for their favorites and consider using a pocket tape recorder to help you remember them.

Make up songs! The easiest way to compose songs is to take a familiar tune and add new words to it. For example, a group of students from a teacher education class made up this song to the tune of "Twinkle, Twinkle, Little Star."

Caterpillar

How can teachers combine songs with whole-language activities?

Since many songs are repetitive or predictable, they serve the same function as predictable books—as a source of whole-language activities. Teachers can make interactive charts, big books, class books, and sentence fill-ins based on songs. Research by Sharon Harris Griffin shows that children attended more to whole-language activities that were extensions of songs than those based on books or classroom activities such as cooking.[2] See the individual activities in this book for many examples of these whole-language activities.

How can teachers use songs to address the special needs of inclusion children?

Teachers can select or create songs that meet the Individual Educational Plan (IEP) goals of some inclusion children. For example, teachers can include songs with directions to increase the vocabulary of children with cognitive or language delays. Teachers can also emphasize through songs the target sounds of children with articulation difficulties. Activity 2.17 shows how specific sounds can be practiced in a song format. Songs often help children with attentional problems stay focused and relaxed.

How can teachers accompany songs?

The autoharp is ideal for teachers to use because they need no musical training in order to play it. Since the autoharp is held on the lap, the teacher can sit on the floor with the children gathered around. The autoharp does not impose the physical barrier between teacher and young children that a piano does; therefore, it reduces management problems and fosters a more intimate relationship between teacher and children. Since autoharps are portable, teachers can use them both inside and out, move them to various parts of the classroom, and even take them along on field trips.

How is the autoharp played?

Since teachers can match letters, they can quickly learn to play the autoharp. The autoharp is held flat on the lap. The left hand is used to press the button labeled with the corresponding letter above the music (for example, the Cs, Fs, and Gs in the "Caterpillar" song). The right hand crosses over the left to strum the strings from bottom to top. Each time the letter above the music changes, the performer presses the matching letter on the autoharp. Typically, people playing the autoharp strum on the beats or when the chords change, as indicated by the letters in the music. With a little bit of practice, teachers can remember the chords without looking at the music. They can experiment with fancier strumming once they are comfortable with the autoharp. Autoharp chords are included in all the songs in this book.

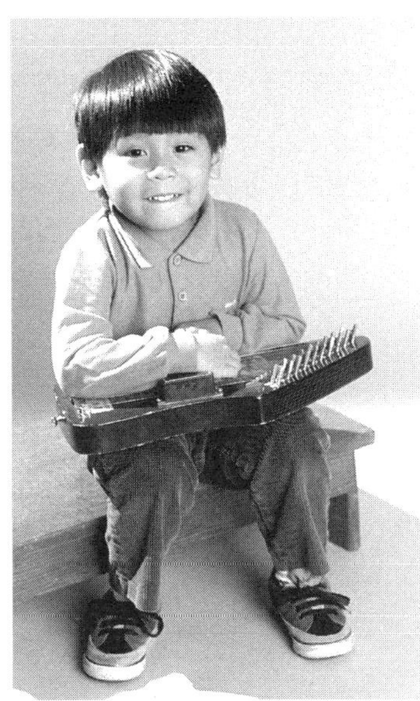

Children can play the autoharp too. First they need to explore and experiment. Older preschool and kindergarten children who have had experience with the autoharp can begin to match the letters on song sheets to the autoharp buttons and also begin to accompany songs. A small rubber spatula makes a good strumming device for children because it is easier to hold than a pick.

How are autoharps tuned?

Each string of the autoharp is labeled with a letter that corresponds to a letter on a tuning device such as a pitch pipe. Pitch pipes are inexpensive. The teacher blows a note on the pitch pipe and turns the corresponding string on the autoharp until the sounds match. Tuning hammers for turning the strings come with most autoharps. Teachers who play another instrument, such as a piano, can tune the autoharp to that instrument.

Endnotes

1. You can order a catalog of Native American educational materials from Oyate, 2702 Mathews Street, Berkeley, CA 94702. The cost of the 1996 catalog was $3.
2. Sharon F. Harris, "A Case Study Approach to the Formative Evaluation of a Curriculum to Support the Growth in Literacy in Three, Four, and Five Year Old Children" (Ph.D. Dissertation, Miami University, 1985).

Song Activities

2.1 Rockabye, Lullaby

Sally Moomaw
© 1996

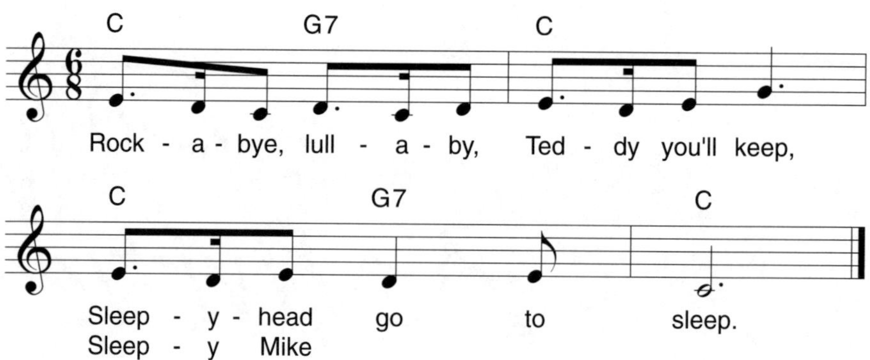

Child's Level

This song is appropriate for toddlers or very young preschoolers.

Why Appropriate

The song is very short, so even toddlers can remember the words.
The text appeals to young children.
The narrow melodic range fits very young voices.
Children's names can be added to the song.

Musical Extension

Children enjoy swaying back and forth to the music as they pretend to rock their teddy bears.

Whole-Language Extension–Interactive Chart

Materials

- ▲ white poster board, 26 by 18 inches
- ▲ pastel sentence strips
- ▲ illustration of child sleeping
- ▲ cards with each child's name made from 8-inch lengths of sentence strips

Description

Young children enjoy adding their names to this chart as they sing the song. Print the words to the song on sentence strips and mount them to the poster board with rubber cement. An attractive illustration draws children's attention to the chart. Laminate the chart. Add a paper fastener to hold the cards with the children's names.

Integrated Curriculum Activities

Read sleepy time books, such as *K Is for Kiss Goodnight,* by Jill Sardegna, and *The Cuddlers,* by Stacy Towle Morgan.

Add teddy bear counters to the manipulative area.

Make a teddy bear grid game for math. See activity 4.7 in *More Than Counting: Whole Math Activities for Preschool and Kindergarten,* by Sally Moomaw and Brenda Hieronymus.

Place teddy bear shaped ice balls in the water table. Children can scoop them up with fish nets.

2.2 Birdie

Sally Moomaw
© 1996

C G7 C

Chirp, chirp, chirp. Bird - ie in your nest.
Chirp, chirp, chirp in the tree that you like best.

Child's Level

This song is most appropriate for toddlers or very young preschoolers.

Why Appropriate

The song is very short and repetitive.
The narrow range fits young voices.
Young children have seen birds and are interested in them.
Children can extend the song by adding the names of specific birds to replace the word *birdie*.

Musical Extension

Clap the beats as you sing, and later add wood blocks (see activity 4.1).

Whole-Language Extension–Interactive Chart

Materials

- ▲ red poster board (or color desired), 22 by 15 inches
- ▲ 2 sentence strips
- ▲ bird illustration
- ▲ bird stickers for word cards

Description

Even very young children enjoy interacting with print as they add the names of familiar birds to this song. Print the words on sentence strips, as shown. Make word cards of types of birds found in your area. Children can hang these word strips on the chart to replace the word *birdie*. Stickers of birds mounted on the cards help children identify the words. Laminate the chart and the cards.

Integrated Curriculum Activities

Put bird nests in the science area, if appropriate for your group.

Read simple books about birds, such as *Goodnight Owl,* by Pat Hutchins, *Flap Your Wings and Try,* by Charlotte Pomerantz, *Bird,* by Moira Butterfield, and *The Big Fat Worm,* by Nancy Van Laan.

2.3 Fire Truck's on the Way

Sally Moomaw
© 1996

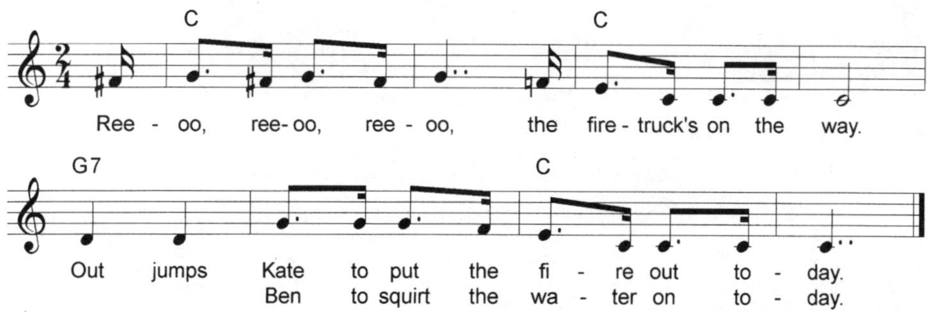

Child's Level

This song appeals to both preschool and kindergarten children because they can put their own names into the song and change the last line to indicate what they would do as firefighters.

Why Appropriate

Children can create their own verses for the song.
The narrow melodic range fits young voices.
The subject matter is of high interest to young children.

Musical Extension

Children can create the fire bell sound by playing triangles on the "ree-oo" syllables.

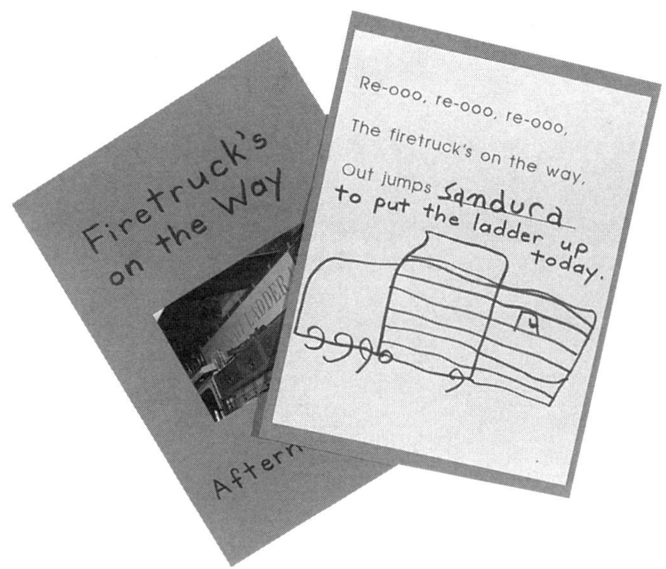

Whole-Language Extension—Class Book

Materials

- ▲ song sheets with the words to the first three lines, minus the child's name, clearly printed
- ▲ markers, crayons, or colored pencils
- ▲ construction paper for front and back covers

Description

Each child can add his or her name to a page of the book. They can either dictate or write a fourth line for the song that tells what they will do as a firefighter.

Integrated Curriculum Activities

Take a trip to a fire station. Use photographs of the children to illustrate a class book.

Read books about firefighters, such as *I'm Going To Be a Firefighter,* by Edith Kunhardt, and *I Can Be a Firefighter,* by Rebecca Hankin.

Put fire trucks in the block area.

Add fire hats, boots, raincoats, and hoses to the dramatic play area. Use a large rectangular box or hollow blocks for a fire truck.

2.4 3 Little Bats

Sally Moomaw

Child's Level

This song is most appropriate for three and four year olds, although young kindergarten children also enjoy deciding how many bats to put on the tree for each line of the song. Additional bats can be added for older children.

Why Appropriate

The words and melody repeat.
The song encourages children to think about number.
The narrow range fits young voices.

Musical Extension

Children can highlight the "E" sounds in the song by playing an instrument, such as triangles, just on those syllables.

Whole-Language Extension—Interactive Chart

Materials

- ▲ poster board, 22 by 18 inches
- ▲ movable bat pieces made of felt and attached to the chart with magnetic tape
- ▲ sentence strips
- ▲ black poster board for the tree

Description

Print the words to the song on sentence strips, as shown, and mount them to the poster board. Cut out a tree shape from black poster board and add it to the right side of the chart. After the chart is laminated, add strips of magnetic tape to the tree branches. Attach pieces of magnetic tape to the backs of the bats. Children can decide how many bats to hang on each branch of the tree. Be sure that the strips of magnetic tape on the branches are all the same length so that children have to figure out for themselves how many bats to put on each branch.

Integrated Curriculum Activities

Include the books *Stellaluna,* by Janell Cannon, and *Bat Time,* by Ruth Horowitz, in the reading area.

Let children dramatize the song.

Include bat-shaped blank books and pencils with bat eraser tops in the writing center.

2.5 Autumn Leaves

Gail Westendorf Klayman
Used by permission

Additional verses

2. Autumn leaves are turning colors . . .
3. Autumn leaves are blowing . . .
4. Autumn leaves are being raked . . .

Child's Level

This song is appropriate for preschool or kindergarten children. Use the additional verses with older preschool or kindergarten children. Children can also make up their own verses.

Why Appropriate

The words describe what children observe in the fall in many parts of the country.

Both words and melody repeat.

The narrow range fits young voices.

Musical Extension

Children can imitate the movements of leaves falling, blowing, and dancing as the song is sung. Have children drop leaves and watch them fall before they imitate the movements. Children can use maracas to create the swishing sound of the leaves.

Whole-Language Extension–Interactive Chart

Materials

- ▲ black poster board, 22 by 22 inches
- ▲ 4 white sentence strips
- ▲ leaf-shaped cut-outs in red, orange, yellow, and brown

Description

Children can hang colored leaves on the chart to change the word *autumn* into the colors of the leaves. Print the words to the song on the sentence strips, as shown. Leave a blank space for the word *autumn*. This is where children will hang the colored leaves. After the chart and leaves are laminated, insert paper fasteners to hold the leaves, or use Velcro or magnetic tape.

Integrated Curriculum Activities

Read autumn books, such as *Red Leaf, Yellow* and *Nuts to You!*, both by Lois Ehlert.

Take a nature walk and collect fall items to use as collage material.

Put buckets, tongs, and nuts from your part of the country in the sensory table.

Place a nut collection for sorting in the manipulative area (see *More Than Counting,* by Sally Moomaw and Brenda Hieronymus, activity 3.15).

Make autumn math games (see *More Than Counting,* by Sally Moomaw and Brenda Hieronymus, activities 4.6, 4.13, and 5.12).

2.6 It Was Snow

Sally Moomaw
© 1978, 1980

Child's Level

This song is appropriate for young preschoolers. The addition of *snow* words in other languages makes it of high interest to older preschool and kindergarten children as well.

Why Appropriate

The song is multicultural.
The repetitive melody and text are easy to remember.
The narrow melodic range is easy for young children to sing.
Children are interested in snow.

Musical Extension

Add finger cymbals for accompaniment once children have had experience clapping the beats.

Snow words in other languages:

Chinese
pronounced *shreh*

Hebrew
pronounced *sheleg*

Thai
pronounced *hee-ma*

Urdu
pronounced *baraf*

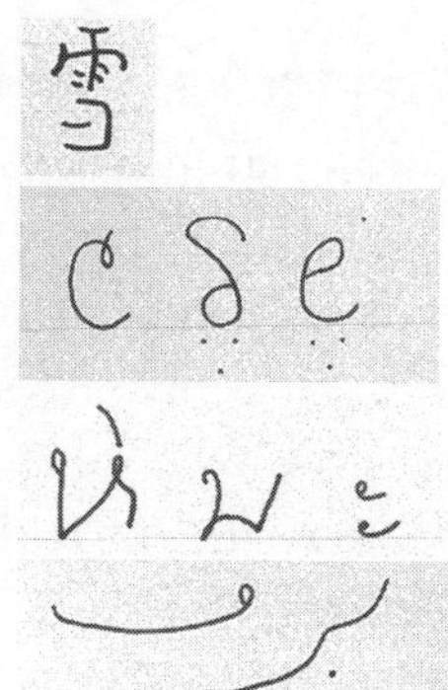

Whole-Language Extension—Big Book

Materials

- ▲ 6 pieces of poster board in assorted shades of blue, 12 by 18 inches each
- ▲ sentence strips
- ▲ cotton balls, construction paper cut-outs, and snowflake stickers to use as illustrations

Description

One line of the song is printed on each page of the book. Since cotton balls are used to illustrate the first page, "It looked like balls of cotton," the pages are covered with clear contact paper rather than laminated. For the final line of the song, attach a pocket made of clear acetate or laminating film. Insert sentence strips with snow written in other languages into the pocket.

Integrated Curriculum Activities

Read books about snow, such as *In the Snow,* by Huy Voun Lee, *Snow on Snow on Snow,* by Cheryl Chapman, *The Snowy Day,* by Ezra Jack Keats, and *Footprints in the Snow,* by Cynthia Benjamin.

Make ink blot pictures using white paint on dark blue or black construction paper.

Bring snow into the classroom! Put it in the sensory table with shovels and buckets.

Spray paint the snow outside with colored water.

2.7 My Special Friend

Sally Moomaw
© 1982, 1996

Child's Level

This song is most appropriate for preschool children, although kindergartners also enjoy singing about their teddy bears or special toys.

Why Appropriate

Children respond readily to the nurturant subject matter. Children can add their own favorite toys to the song.

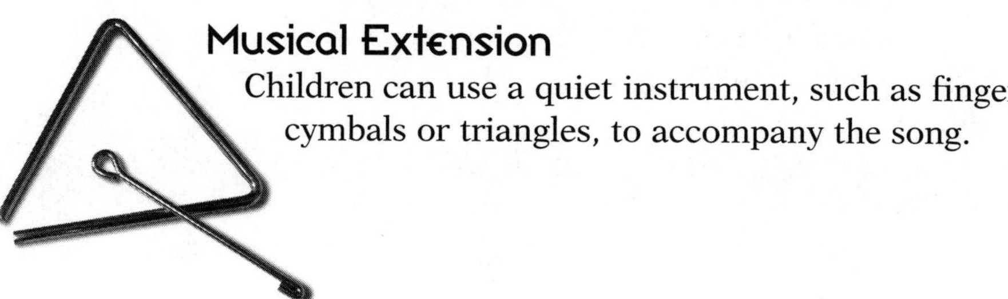

Musical Extension

Children can use a quiet instrument, such as finger cymbals or triangles, to accompany the song.

Whole-Language Extension–Class Book

Materials

- ▲ white construction paper, 12 by 18 inches
- ▲ markers
- ▲ felt scraps and cotton balls
- ▲ glue

Description

Children can transform the song into a surprise flap book. Fold the construction paper in half and print the first three lines of the song on the flap. The children can lift up the flaps and create their special friend by cutting and gluing felt and cotton or by drawing. Children can dictate or write a last line for the song that includes their favorite toy. Punch holes in the left-hand side of the paper and mount the pages on rings, or bind the book with a spiral binder.

Integrated Curriculum Activities

Read books about teddy bears or special toys, such as *When the Teddy Bears Came,* by Martin Waddell, and *A Pocket for Corduroy,* by Don Freeman.

Use a teddy bear poem for a rhythm activity (see activity 3.8).

Put teddy bear counters with a balance scale in the science area to experiment with weight.

2.8 Clouds

words by Peter Moomaw
music by Sally Moomaw

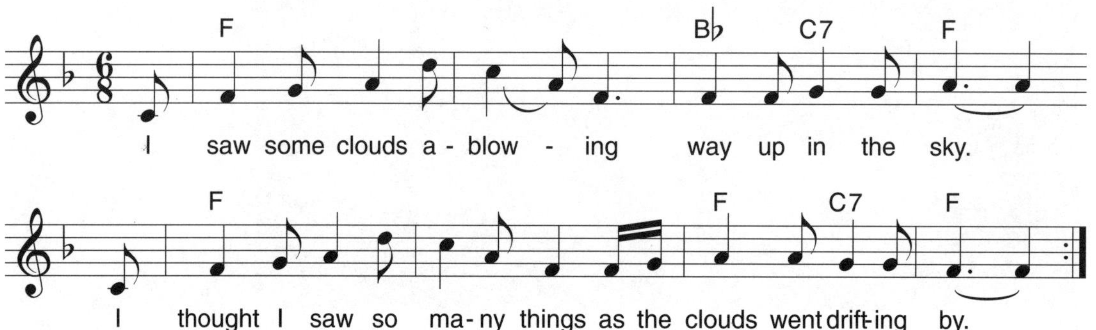

I thought I saw a horsy way up in the sky.
I thought I saw a horsy as the clouds went drifting by.

I thought I saw a great big crane way up in the sky.
I thought I saw a great big crane as the clouds went drifting by.

The sky man drove the crane away way up in the sky.
The sky man drove the crane away as the clouds went drifting by.

Child's Level

This song is appropriate for both preschool and kindergarten children.

Why Appropriate

Children can use their imaginations to alter the words of the song and add the shapes they see in clouds.

The words and melody repeat.

Musical Extension

Children can use rainsticks to accompany this song (see activity 5.6 for a description of the instrument). If you have several rainsticks, a few children can play at a time. As you repeat the song and allow children to add additional words for the cloud shapes, the children can pass the instruments around until everyone has had a turn. You can also make maracas. Use clear plastic jars or bottles so the children can see what produces the sound, and fill them with rice or sand. These also create a soft, breezy accompaniment.

Whole-Language Extension—Interactive Chart

Materials

- ▲ royal blue poster board, 22 by 28 inches
- ▲ cloud illustration (look for one in magazines)
- ▲ white paint marker
- ▲ white cut-outs to represent the shapes of clouds children describe

Description

Print the words to the song on the poster board, as pictured. Use the cloud image as an illustration to draw interest to the chart. Cut out shapes from white paper to represent the forms children say the clouds may take. These are the interactive pieces, which could be coordinated with the book *It Looked Like Spilt Milk,* by Charles G. Shaw. This predictable book shows many shapes clouds might take. After the chart and pieces are laminated, attach a paper fastener at the end of the first line to hold the cloud shapes to the chart. Magnetic tape or Velcro can also be used.

Integrated Curriculum Activities

Read books about clouds and weather, such as *It Looked Like Spilt Milk,* by Charles G. Shaw, *The Wind Blew,* by Pat Hutchins, and *The Cloud Book,* by Tomie de Paola.

Give the children pieces of white fiberfill so they can create cloud shapes as they sing the song.

Put white pompoms in blue water in the sensory table. Children can fish them out with tongs.

Make cloud pictures by putting white paint on dark blue paper and letting the children blow the paint with straws.

2.9 Hurry Mama

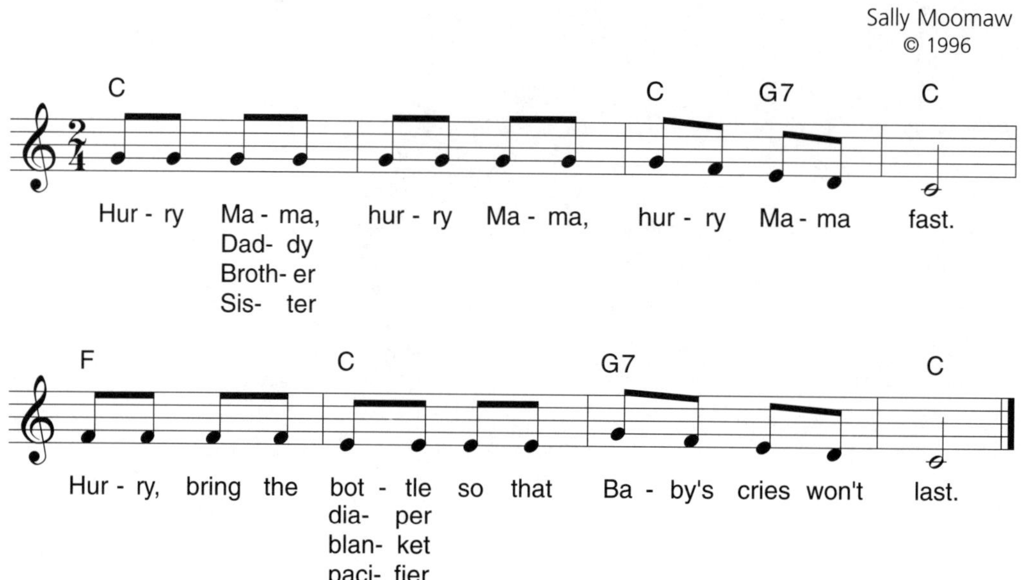

Child's Level

This song appeals to both preschool and kindergarten children. They enjoy adding their own ideas to the song for what Baby needs and who will bring it.

Why Appropriate

The subject is appealing to young children, who often have younger siblings at home.

The repetitive melody and text are easy for young children to remember.

The narrow melodic range fits young voices.

Musical Extension

Children can accompany the song by using baby rattles for maracas. Ask parents for donations.

Whole-Language Extension–Class Book

Materials

- ▲ songs sheets with the words to the song clearly printed, but with blank spaces for children to fill in who will bring something to the baby and what they will bring
- ▲ markers, crayons, or colored pencils

Description

Each child can decide what Baby needs and who will bring it, and their words can be added to the song. Children can write their ideas themselves or dictate the words to an adult. The children can illustrate their pages. The pages are stapled together to form a class book that can be placed on the bookshelf and sung at group time.

Integrated Curriculum Activities

Read books about babies, such as *More More More, Said the Baby,* by Vera B. Williams, *Sleep, Sleep, Sleep,* by Nancy Van Laan, *Welcoming Babies,* by Margy Burns Knight, and *Peter's Chair,* by Ezra Jack Keats.

Make baby cereal with the children and taste baby food.

Add multicultural baby dolls, diapers, bottles, baby clothes, and infant toys to the dramatic play area.

Wash baby dolls in the sensory table.

Make a math game with a baby theme (see *More Than Counting,* by Sally Moomaw and Brenda Hieronymus, activity 4.17).

2.10 Thunder

Sally Moomaw
© 1978, 1980

Additional verses

2. I looked up in the sky and saw a FLASH, FLASH, FLASH,
   I covered up my ears to stop the CRASH, CRASH, CRASH.
   My daddy said, "Don't worry 'bout the SPLASH, SPLASH, SPLASH,
   It only means that now it's time to DASH, DASH, DASH!"

3. I looked up in the sky and saw the RAIN STREAK DOWN,
   A hundred little rivers on the GROUND, GROUND, GROUND.
   My daddy said, "Don't worry 'bout the FLOOD, FLOOD, FLOOD,
   For soon we will go wading in the MUD, MUD, MUD!"

4. I looked up in the sky and saw a DOUBLE RAINBOW,
   I didn't want the colors to ever GO, GO, GO.
   My daddy said, "Don't worry when they FADE AWAY,
   I've taken us a picture for ANOTHER DAY!"

Child's Level

This song is most appropriate for older preschool or kindergarten children.

Why Appropriate

The song helps relieve children's fears about storms.
The repetition of the melody and words make the song easier for children to learn and remember.
The melodic range is narrow and therefore easier for young voices to sing.

Musical Extension

Have children play cymbals or drums on the words in capital letters at the end of each line to create the sound of thunder.

Whole-Language Extension–Big Book

Materials

- ▲ 8 pieces of white construction paper, 12 by 18 inches each
- ▲ sentence strips
- ▲ magazine cut-outs or drawings to illustrate the words

Description

The predictable nature of the "Thunder" song makes it appropriate for a big book. Print the words to the song on sentence strips and mount them to the construction paper with rubber cement. Allow two pages of the book for each line of the song. Illustrate the book pages with stickers, magazine cut-outs, or drawings. Laminate the pages or cover with clear contact paper.

Integrated Curriculum Activities

Place rainsticks in the music area (see activity 5.6).
Include the books *Umbrella,* by Taro Yashima, *The Napping House,* by Audrey Wood, *Hurricane,* by David Wiesner, and *Rain,* from Wonder Books, in the reading area.
Make raindrop finger puppets out of felt.
Create pictures using colored water and eyedroppers.

2.11 Bingo, Revisited

words by Sally Moomaw
Traditional melody
Lyrics © 1996

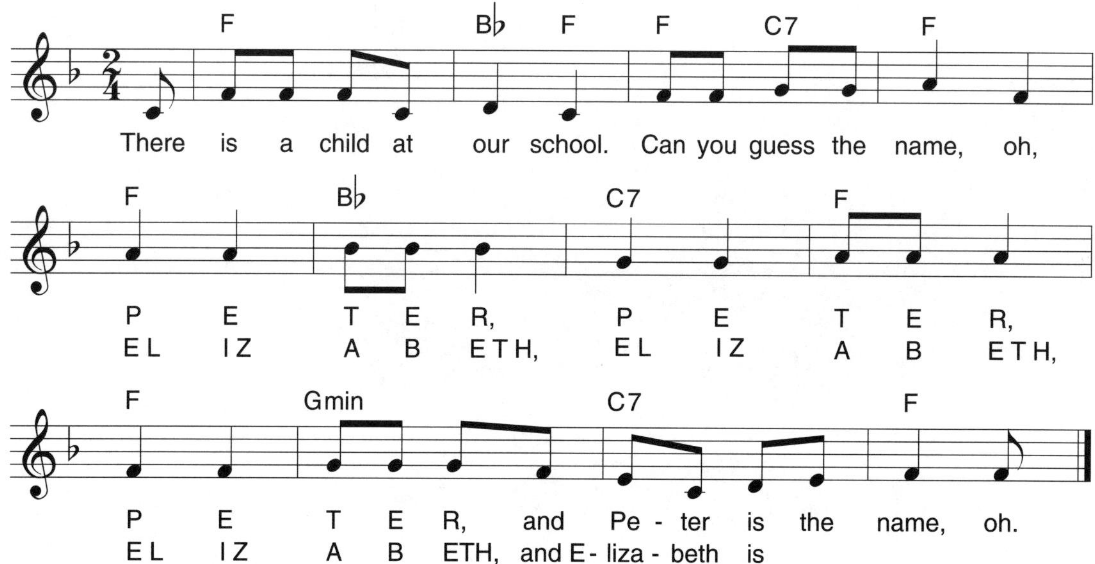

Child's Level

This song is appropriate for older preschool or kindergarten children.

Why Appropriate

Children love to hear their own names spelled out in this familiar song.

There is extensive repetition of words, letters, and melody.

Musical Extension

Use wood blocks to play the letters of each child's name after the children have learned to clap them.

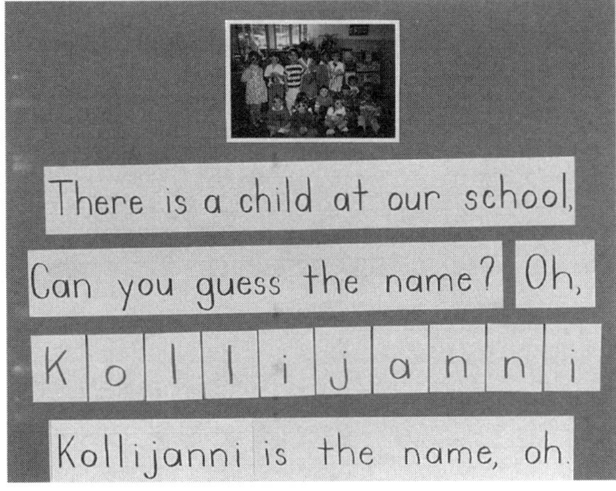

Whole-Language Extension—Interactive Chart

Materials

- ▲ colored poster board, 22 by 28 inches
- ▲ white sentence strips
- ▲ magnetic tape
- ▲ white index cards, 3 by 5 inches, cut in half (3 by 2½ inches)
- ▲ class photo

Description

Print the words to the song on the sentence strips, as pictured, and print the letters to each child's name on the index cards, with one letter per card. Mount the sentence strips to the chart with rubber cement, but leave enough space at the top of the chart for the class photo, and allow 4-inches of space between lines two and four to hold the letter cards. Laminate the chart and the letter cards. Mount the class photo at the top of the chart with magnetic tape. This allows you to change the picture if you have more than one class or for succeeding years. Put a strip of magnetic tape across the chart in the space left for line three. Mount pieces of magnetic tape to the back of the letter cards so the children can hang the letters to their names on the chart. They can also add sentence strips with their names to the beginning of line four.

Integrated Curriculum Activities

Read alphabet books, such as *K Is for Kiss Goodnight,* by Jill Sardegna, *A Is for Aloha,* by Stephanie Feeney, *Navajo ABC,* by Luci Tapahonso and Eleanor Schick, and *Chicka, Chicka, Boom Boom,* by Bill Martin Jr. and John Archambault.

Put alphabet puzzles in the manipulative area.

Put foam letters and Plexiglas easels in the water table. Children can adhere the letters to the easels.

Use alphabet cookie cutters with playdough.

2.12 Lullaby World

Sally Moomaw

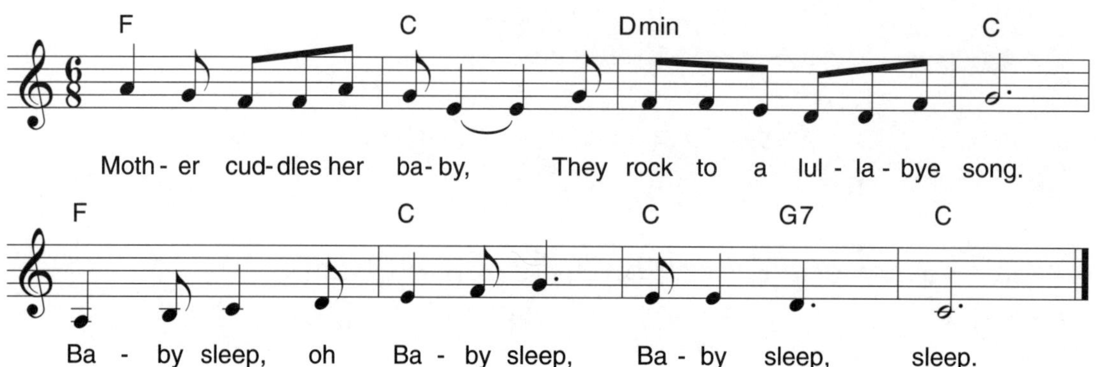

Child's Level

This song is most appropriate for older preschool and kindergarten children, who find the words in other languages challenging and exciting.

Why Appropriate

The melody has a wider range for somewhat older children.

The nurturant subject matter comforts young children.

Including words from other languages for *baby* and *sleep* conveys the idea that mothers from around the world love and nurture their babies.

Musical Extension

Children can play finger cymbals softly on the beats to convey the soft sounds of sleep.

"Baby sleep, sleep" in other languages:

Cambodian
pronounced *goan nga dake, dake* កូនងា ទៅដេក ទៅដេក

Korean
pronounced *Agah, Ja Jahng, Ja Jahng* 아가 자장 자장

Indonesian
Bayi, tidurlah, tidurlah

Spanish
El niño, duerme, duerme

Whole-Language Extension–Big Book

Materials

- ▲ 6 sheets of pale blue construction paper (or color desired), 12 by 18 inches each
- ▲ sentence strips (pink, or color desired)
- ▲ illustrations of babies and mothers, preferably multicultural

Description

Print the words to the song on the sentence strips and use rubber cement to mount them on the construction paper. Six pieces of construction paper are enough for one page for each line of the song, plus a front and back cover. Illustrate with pictures of babies and mothers. Once the pages are laminated, mount a strip of clear lamination across the last line of the song ("Baby sleep, sleep") to form a pocket. Write these words in other languages to add to the song (parents from your school or community are an excellent resource).

Integrated Curriculum Activities

Include pictures of mothers and babies from many cultures in the classroom.

Play tapes of lullabies in many languages, such as *The World Sings Goodnight*.

Read books that illustrate mothers and fathers nurturing their babies, such as *I Love My Mommy Because . . .* and *I Love My Daddy Because . . .* , both by Laurel Porter-Gaylord, *Sleep, Sleep, Sleep,* by Nancy Van Laan, and *Before I Was Born,* by Harriet Ziefert.

2.13 Hush, Little Baby

Traditional

Additional verses

And if that mockingbird won't sing,
Papa's gonna buy you a diamond ring.

And if that diamond ring turns to brass,
Papa's gonna buy you a looking glass.

And if that looking glass gets broke,
Papa's gonna buy you a billy goat.

And if that billy goat won't pull,
Papa's gonna buy you a cart and bull.

And if that cart and bull turn over,
Papa's gonna buy you a dog named Rover.

And if that dog named Rover won't bark,
Papa's gonna buy you a horse and cart.

And if that horse and cart fall down,
You'll still be the sweetest little baby in town.

Child's Level

This song is most appropriate for older preschool and kindergarten children because of its longer length.

Why Appropriate

The text reinforces over and over a father's unconditional love for his child.

The rhyming words are especially appropriate for the language development of four and five year olds.

The melody is easy to sing.

Musical Extension

Children can accompany the song by using baby rattles for maracas. Ask parents for donations.

Whole-Language Extension–Interactive Chart

Materials

- ▲ light blue poster board (or color desired), 20 by 22 inches,
- ▲ photographs of babies, preferably multicultural
- ▲ sentence strips

Description

Print the words to the song on sentence strips, as pictured, and mount the sentence strips to the poster board with rubber cement. Use baby pictures to illustrate the chart and draw children's attention to it. After the chart is laminated, attach a strip of clear laminating film to form a pocket for the last line of the chart. The words for the gifts Papa gives Baby are printed on sentence strips. Children can put them into the pocket of the chart for line four as they sing the verses of the song. The children's names can be written on sentence strips and added to the chart to replace the word *baby* on line one. They can be held in place with a paper fastener or magnetic tape.

Integrated Curriculum Activities

Include a book version of the song, such as *Hush, Little Baby,* by Aliki, in the book area.

Read other books about babies, such as *Hush!,* by Minfong Ho, and *Sleep, Sleep, Sleep,* by Nancy Van Laan.

Wash baby dolls or baby clothes in the water table.

Have the children taste baby food and graph the results.

Add multicultural dolls, diapers, toys, and baby clothes to the dramatic play area.

2.14 Tornado

Sally Moomaw
© 1979, 1996

Child's Level

This song is most appropriate for older preschool and kindergarten children.

Why Appropriate

The song helps children who live in areas where tornadoes are common to express their fears and to understand tornadoes. The words to the song reflect the actual words that young children use to describe tornadoes. Children respond eagerly to the song by discussing where they go at home and school to be safe during severe storms.

Musical Extension

Children may wish to use cymbals to re-create the sound of thunder that often accompanies storms.

Whole-Language Extension—Big Book

Materials

- 10 pieces of black construction paper, 12 by 18 inches each
- sentence strips
- drawings or magazine pictures of tornadoes for illustrations, one family picture to illustrate line seven ("We'll go into a safe place"), a picture of a clear sky for line eight ("Until it passes by")

Description

Ten pieces of construction paper are enough for one page for each line of the song, plus a front and back cover. Print the words to the song on sentence strips and mount them to the construction paper with rubber cement. Allow one line of the song per page. Illustrate the pages with magazine pictures, or paint tornado shapes with gray tempera paint. Illustrate line seven with a picture of a family, and illustrate the last line with a picture of a clear sky. This emphasizes that the storm ends. Laminate the pages. You may wish to mount a clear pocket made from extra laminating film over the words *safe place* on line seven. Children can write or dictate where they go at home to seek safety from tornadoes, such as a basement, and add them to the song.

Integrated Curriculum Activities

Read weather-related books, such as *Hurricane,* by David Wiesner. Put funnels in the water table.

2.15 Swish, Swish, Swish

Sally Moomaw

Additional verses

1. Swish, swish, swish,
   Four little fish,
   Swimming through the water,
   Swish, swish, swish.

2. Swish, swish, swish,
   One little fish gets
   Caught in a *rock,*
   Swish, swish, swish. Ouch!

3. Swish, swish, swish,
   One little fish gets
   Caught in a *shipwreck,*
   Swish, swish, swish. Ouch!

4. Swish, swish, swish,
   One little fish gets
   Caught in a *fishing net,*
   Swish, swish, swish. Ouch!

Child's Level

This song suits a range of children. Verse one is appropriate for toddlers or young preschoolers. Older preschool and kindergarten children enjoy the additional verses, especially when the song is coordinated with the predictable book *Blue Sea,* by Robert Kalan.

Why Appropriate

The repetitive text and melody are easy to remember.
The topic is interesting to young children.
The narrow melodic range fits young voices.

Musical Extension

Let children accompany the song with water maracas (see activity 4.4 for directions). These maracas sound like water lapping the shore and add an interesting tone color.

Whole-Language Extension–Interactive Chart

for verses two through four

Materials

- ▲ blue poster board, 22 by 22 inches
- ▲ illustration of the four fish cut from orange, pink, green, and yellow construction paper
- ▲ sentence strips

Description

Print one line of the song for each line of the chart. The italicized words of the song are the interactive words; print them on separate pieces of sentence strips. After the chart is laminated, tape a pocket made from extra laminating film to the chart to hold the interactive word cards. Children can write other ideas for how the fish get caught and add them to the chart.

Integrated Curriculum Activities

Put plastic fish and fish nets in the water table.

Consider getting a fish for a class pet.

Put blank books shaped like fish in the writing center along with sea animal word cards.

Put a beach in the dramatic play area. Use a small, plastic wading pool filled with sand and shells for the beach.

Put a shell collection for sorting and classifying in the manipulative area (see *More Than Counting,* by Sally Moomaw and Brenda Hieronymus, activity 3.8).

Use shells in the music area (see activity 4.7).

Read sea books, such as *Blue Sea,* by Robert Kalan, *Swimmy,* by Leo Lionni, *Tough Boris,* by Mem Fox, and *Something Queer on Vacation,* by Elizabeth Levy.

2.16 No Witches

Sally Moomaw
© 1997

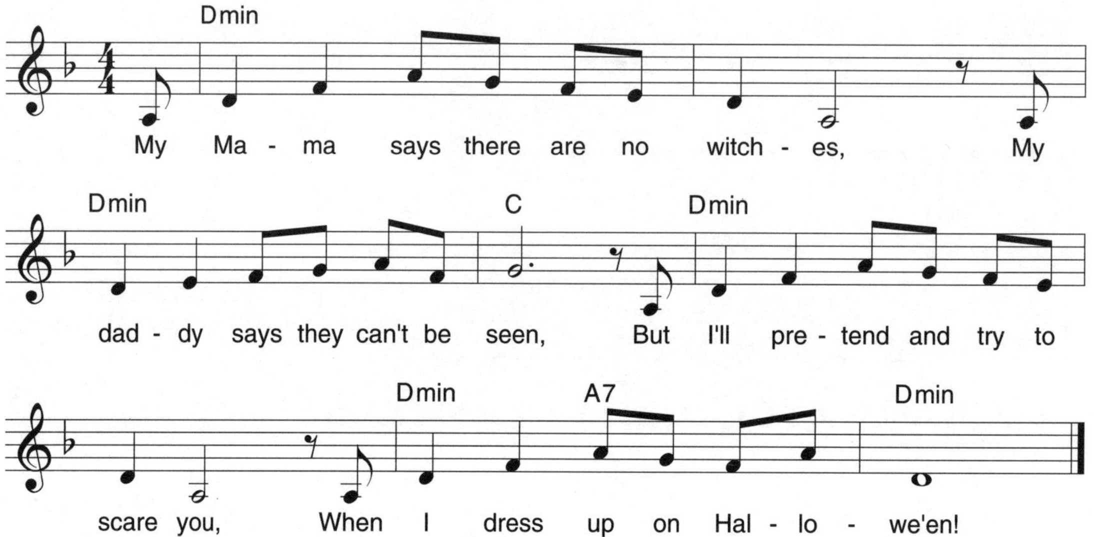

Child's Level

This song is appropriate for older preschool and kindergarten children.

Why Appropriate

Many Halloween songs are frightening to young children. This song emphasizes the pretend nature of costumes and allows children to express their own fears by adding words to the song.

Musical Extension

Let the children accompany the song with kazoos. As they hum into the kazoos, they create a "spooky" sound. This is an excellent activity for children with weak facial muscles. Some children with speech problems or Down syndrome have weak facial muscles.

Whole-Language Extension–Interactive Chart

Materials

- ▲ yellow poster board, 22 by 28 inches
- ▲ drawing or photograph for illustration
- ▲ orange sentence strips

Description

Write the words to the song on the sentence strips, as shown, and mount them to the poster board with rubber cement. Leave a blank space for the word *witches*. After the chart is laminated, attach a pocket made from extra laminating film to the chart in the space where the word *witches* would go. Children can write extra words to add to the song and put them in the pocket. *Ghosts* and *monsters* are typical additions.

Integrated Curriculum Activities

Carefully select books that emphasize the pretend nature of Halloween, such as *Humbug Witch,* by Lorna Balian, and *The Real-Skin Rubber Monster Mask,* by Mirian Cohen.

Estimate the number of grooves on a pumpkin.

Take a trip to a pumpkin farm to see how pumpkins grow.

Put dried gourds in the music area for maracas (see activity 5.4).

2.17 How Does It Go?

(Inclusion Activity)

Sally Moomaw
© 1980

2. How does the car sound when it won't start? k, k, k, k, k.
3. How does the monkey go? Chee, chee, chee.
4. How do the children sing? La, la, la.
5. How does the baby go? d, d, d.
6. How does the race car go? Brum, brum, brum.

Child's Level

This song targets preschool or kindergarten children with articulation difficulties. The specific articulation goals can be incorporated into the song. Although the song is planned with particular children in mind, the whole class enjoys singing it.

Why Appropriate

The melody and words are short and repetitive.
Children enjoy making interesting sounds to illustrate the words.

Musical Extension

No musical extension is recommended. Although children could play rhythm instruments on the sounds, the purpose of the song is to encourage them to create the sounds vocally. Playing instruments might discourage this.

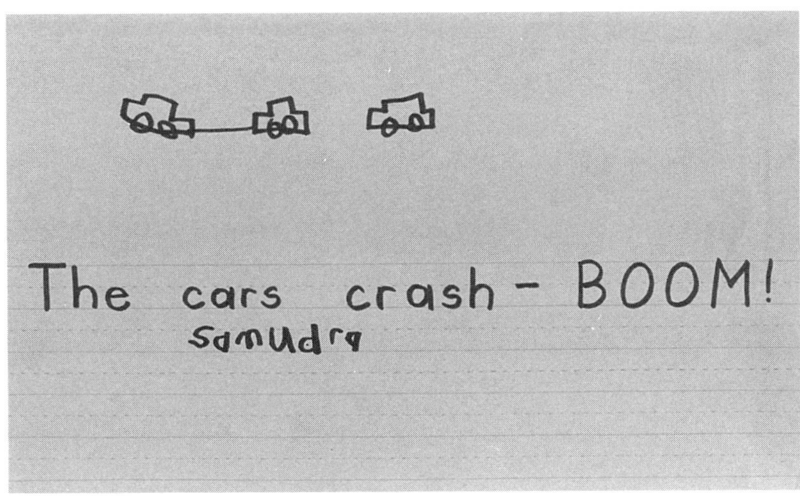

Whole-Language Extension—Class Book

Materials

- ▲ story paper (blank at the top and lined at the bottom), 12 by 18 inches
- ▲ markers

Description

Children can write or dictate stories about interesting sounds from their world. The individual pages can be assembled into a class book.

Integrated Curriculum Activity

Read books about sounds, such as *Max the Music-Maker,* by Miriam B. Stechler and Alice S. Kandell, *Too Much Noise,* by Ann McGovern, *Rat-a-Tat, Pitter Pat,* by Alan Benjamin, and *Barnyard Banter,* by Denise Fleming.

Rhythm

While waiting to come inside from the playground, three children began to chant the name of a fourth child who was still playing on the climber:

Lind-say, Lind-say, Lind-say.

▲ ▲ ▲

Dante sat in the music area of his classroom experimenting with the sounds of several sizes of triangles. Suddenly he began singing "Twinkle, Twinkle, Little Star" and played the beats of the song on one of the triangles.

▲ ▲ ▲

Kim was jumping on a small trampoline in the gross-motor room. Her teacher watched for a while and then began to chant:

Kim, Kim, on the trampoline,
Kim is jumping on the trampoline.

▲ ▲ ▲

Children show a strong feel for rhythm from an early age. Toddlers, preschool children, and kindergartners often respond to the rhythm of music by spontaneously clapping or swaying to the beat. Rhythm is an important component of a comprehensive early childhood music curriculum.

Teachers' Questions

What is rhythm?

Rhythm pertains to patterns of sound perceived in relationship to a recurring beat or pulse. The beat is analogous to a heartbeat or the ticking of a clock. We often find ourselves tapping our feet, clapping our hands, or snapping our fingers to the beat of music.

Superimposed on the framework of this steady pulse are varying patterns of sound that form the actual rhythm of the music.

Why is it important to include rhythm activities in the curriculum?

Children explore rhythm as a natural part of development. As they construct concepts of rhythm, children increase their awareness of the function of rhythm throughout their world, whether in the sounds of language, the feel of music, or the patterns of mathematics, science, and art.

Exploring rhythm through planned activities encourages children to focus their listening. They learn to concentrate on one aspect of sound, such as the beat or a recurring rhythmic pattern, and also hear this rhythm as part of the whole piece of music. Needless to say, this greatly increases children's appreciation and enjoyment of music. Perhaps even more importantly, children widely apply the ability to isolate patterns while still perceiving the whole as they move forward in school and in life. For example, they may tap out syllables when attempting to read long words, focus on rhythmic patterns when learning new languages, or use rhythm as a tool to perceive and remember mathematical patterns (see activity 3.13).

What kinds of rhythmic activities can teachers plan?

Clapping the rhythms in speech is an excellent way for children to begin feeling rhythm. The concept of using speech to develop rhythmic awareness in children was developed by the German composer and educator Carl Orff (1895–1982).

Children can begin by clapping the sounds, or syllables, of familiar words, such as their names. The teacher chants each child's name, in its appropriate rhythm, three or four times. As she says each name, she claps one time for each syllable. Children will quickly wish to join in.

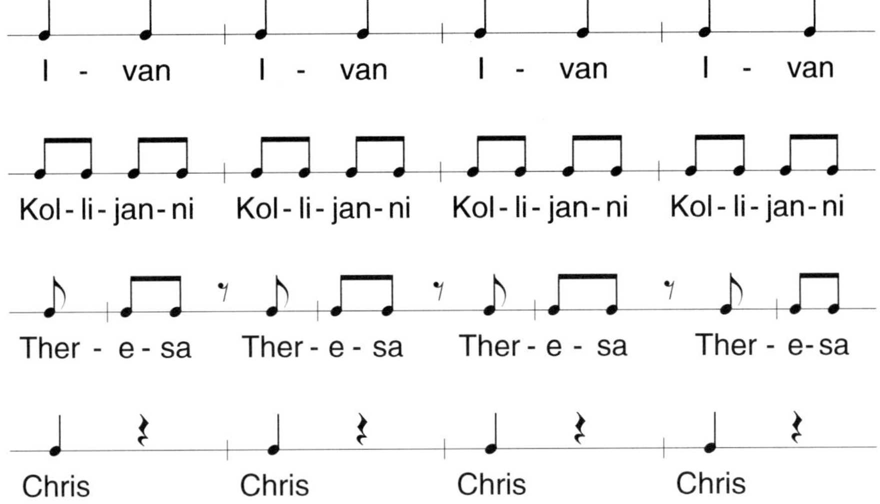

The interpretation of the rhythmic symbols is as follows:

♩ ♩ Clap on each beat.

♫ ♫ When two notes are *beamed* together, clap on each beat and clap again exactly halfway between each beat and the next beat.

𝄾 ♪ The symbol 𝄾 denotes a silence, called a *rest*, for that half-beat. In this example, rest on the first half of the beat and clap on the second half of the beat.

♩ 𝄽 The symbol 𝄽 denotes a *rest* for the entire beat. In this example, clap on the first beat, but do not clap on the second beat.

See activities 3.1, 3.2, and 3.3 for other examples of speech patterns used for rhythmic activities.

Chanting is another good rhythm activity for young children. Chanting involves reciting a poem that has a strong rhythmic feel in a manner that accentuates the beats. Clapping the beats while saying the words helps children gain a feel for the beat.

Chants are used for emphasizing the beat in music because, unlike a song, they do not have a melody. Thus, children can more easily focus on the rhythm since there is no tune to distract them. Once children have developed a feel for the beat in chants, they can go on to clapping the beats in songs. See activities 3.4 through 3.12 for examples of chants.

What criteria should teachers consider when selecting chants?

Teachers should select poems that have a strong rhythm so that children can easily feel the beat. Teachers should also consider the length of the chant and the content of the words.

How long should the chant be?

As with songs, the length of the chant depends on the age of the children. Toddlers need very short, simple chants of about one line in length. Four lines is typical for three and four year olds, while kindergarten children may be ready for longer and more complicated chants. As always, teachers must assess their own groups to determine the appropriate level of difficulty. For whole-language extensions, two to four lines is an ideal amount of print.

What constitutes good content in a chant for young children?

The subject should be relevant to the lives of the children. Topics that are appropriate for songs, such as animals, families, seasons, and vehicles, also make good chants.

The most familiar chants for young children are Mother Goose rhymes. While these rhymes often project a strong rhythm, they originate from a time and place far removed from our children. Children today often have no idea what the words mean. For example, the familiar chant "Peas Porridge" has a strong beat but words that most children today do not understand. The chant "I Can Run" uses the same rhythm but has words that are meaningful to even very young children.

In the chant examples in this book, each beat is notated with a vertical straight line, which is a *quarter note* (♩) without the note head. The rhythmic patterns of the words are not notated because the clapping is done only on each beat, regardless of the number of syllables. Whenever a beat occurs without a syllable, an asterisk (*) is used as a placeholder.

Peas Porridge

Mother Goose

|	|	|	|
Peas	Porridge	hot,	*
|	|	|	|
Peas	Porridge	cold,	*
|	|	|	|
Peas	Porridge	in the	pot
|	|	|	|
Nine	days	old.	*

I Can Run

Sally Moomaw
© 1979, 1980

|	|	|	|
I	can	run,	*
|	|	|	|
I	can	play,	*
|	|	|	|
I	like to	jump &	skip
|	|	|	|
Ev'	-ry	day.	*

Where can teachers find chants?

Teachers can use the words to preexisting songs as chants. Select a song that has a strong rhythmic feel and is an appropriate length. Then, instead of singing the song, chant the words and clap the beats. At a later time you can sing the song if you desire.

Some children's poetry make excellent chants. Keep in mind that not all poetry is meant to be recited rhythmically. Chanting some poems could ruin them aesthetically.

Teachers can also write their own chants. The key is to develop a strongly accented beat in the poem. At first teachers may wish to use a traditional chant such as "Peas Porridge" and change the words while keeping the same rhythm.

What is the best way to teach a chant?

The teacher should rhythmically recite the entire chant several times while clapping the beats. Children should be encouraged to join in by clapping along or saying the words whenever they are ready. As with songs, children quickly lose the overall meaning of a chant when teachers break them into single lines.

At what age do children begin to feel the beat in music?

Many children begin to show a feel for the beat in music at some point during the preschool years. Other children may develop this ability in kindergarten or later. Some children demonstrate a feel for rhythm early in the preschool years, particularly if they come from families that emphasize participation in music-making and the clapping of rhythms.

What should the teacher do when children do not feel the beat?

The teacher should continue to include music activities that emphasize rhythm, such as chants and speech exercises. Children progress in their musical development at varying rates, just as they do in other areas. With continued opportunities to participate in music-making and rhythmic activities, children will continue to increase their rhythmic awareness.

Perhaps more important is what the teacher should not do, and that is to draw attention to children by taking their hands and attempting to assist them in clapping the beats. This does not seem to increase children's rhythmic awareness, but may embarrass them or convey the unintended idea that they are not very good at music. Children may then begin to avoid participating in music activities.

How can teachers make rhythm activities more complex?

Teachers can increase the length of both speech exercises and chants to make them more difficult. They can also replace clapping with rhythm instruments or more complex clapping patterns. For older children, several rhythmic lines can be combined, as in examples 3.13, 3.14, and 3.15.

How can children use instruments in rhythm activities?

Once children become skilled at clapping rhythms and beats, they can begin playing those rhythms or beats on rhythm instruments, such as wood blocks or drums. The strokes on the instrument replace the claps. Teachers should select a single type of instrument for the activity so that the children can clearly hear the rhythmic patterns. The rhythm is quickly obliterated when a variety of instruments are used simultaneously. Also, the instrument selected should make one clear sound per stroke (such as a wood block), as opposed to an instrument such as jingle bells, where the sound is diffuse and tends to muddle the clarity of the rhythm. (You'll find a detailed description of instruments in chapter 4.)

What are some more complex clapping patterns?

Instead of just clapping the beats, more experienced children may want to alternate clapping with patting their thighs or lap. Rhythmic patterns might also involve stamping. Teachers can introduce a variety of patterns when children are ready. Whatever the pattern, the movement is done on the beats. Some examples follow:

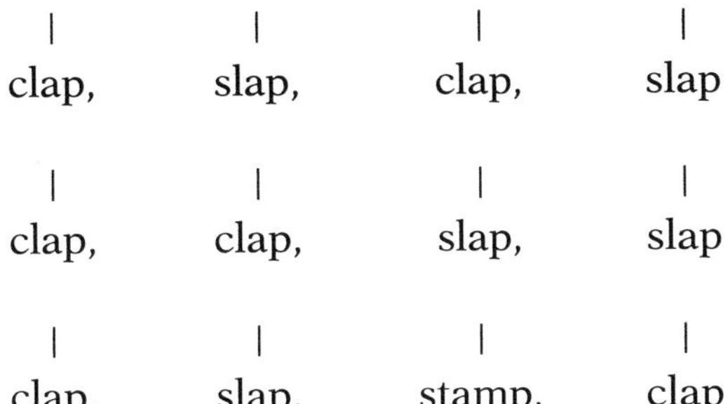

What is an ostinato?

An ostinato *is a repeating pattern; a rhythmic ostinato is a repeating rhythmic pattern.* Ostinati can range from very simple, such as clapping a steady beat, to long and complex. They can be clapped or played on rhythm instruments and can be used to accompany speech exercises or chants. Ostinati can also be used in combination with other rhythmic ostinati. The clapping patterns described earlier in this chapter are examples of one type of rhythmic ostinati. Rhythmic ostinati are used in some of the rhythm activities in this chapter (see activities 3.13, 3.14, and 3.15).

How can teachers combine chants with whole-language or whole-math activities?

Chants are usually short, repetitive, and predictable. This makes them ideal for whole-language extensions. Teachers can use chants for big books, interactive charts, and sentence fill-ins. See the activities in this chapter for ideas for whole-language extensions. Some rhythmic activities are ideal for facilitating children's construction of math concepts such as quantification, subtraction, and patterning. See activities 3.10 and 3.13 for examples.

Rhythm Activities

3.1 Class Names

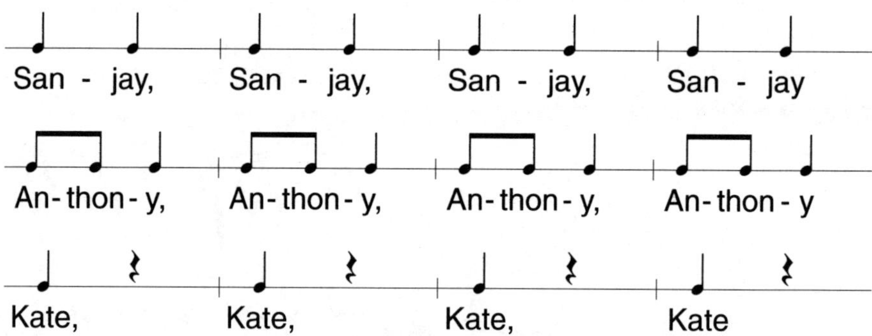

Description

Say each child's name rhythmically, and then repeat the name several times while clapping each syllable.

Child's Level

Clapping names is appropriate for children from early preschool through kindergarten. It is an excellent first rhythm activity since children love focusing on their names.

Why Appropriate

Children are especially interested in their own names and the names of their classmates.

Clapping the syllables emphasizes the rhythmic patterns of language.

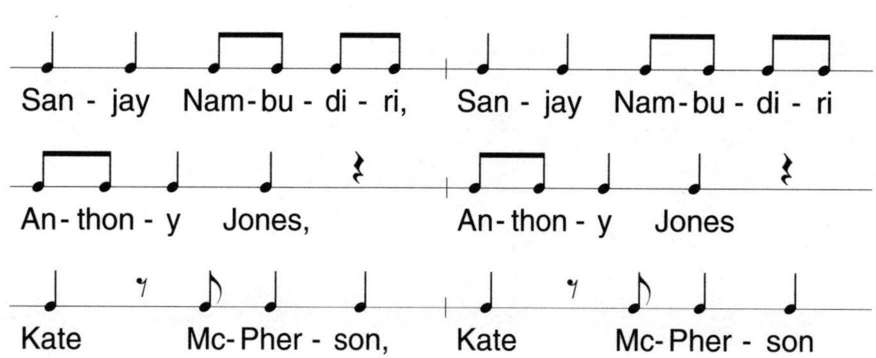

Modification

Once children have become adept at clapping their first names, increase the difficulty by clapping both first and last names.

Musical Extension

Have children play a rhythm instrument, such as wood blocks, on each syllable to replace the claps.

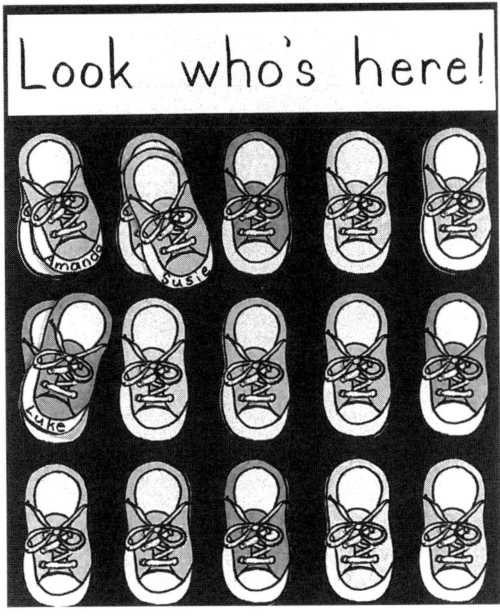

Whole-Language Extension—Class Attendance Chart

Materials

- ▲ poster board, 16 by 22 inches (or a size large enough to hold a shape for each child in the class)
- ▲ shape cut-outs (twice as many as the number of children in the class)
- ▲ sentence strip
- ▲ paper fasteners

Description

Children can participate in taking attendance with this chart. Write the words "Look who's here!" on the sentence strip and mount it at the top of the poster board. Color the shape cut-outs as desired and glue one set to the poster board with rubber cement. Print each child's name on the remaining shapes. Laminate both the board and the shapes. Add a paper fastener to each shape on the board. Children can find their name tags as they enter class each day and hang them on the board. You can refer to the chart when you lead the name clapping activity.

Integrated Curriculum Activities

Sing songs with the children's names, such as "Where, Oh Where?" (activity 7.7) and "Bingo, Revisited" (activity 2.11).

Read books about friends, such as *My Best Friend,* by Pat Hutchins, *A Letter to Amy,* by Ezra Jack Keats, and *My Friends,* by Taro Gomi.

Add word cards with the names of the children in the class to the writing center.

3.2 Dinosaurs

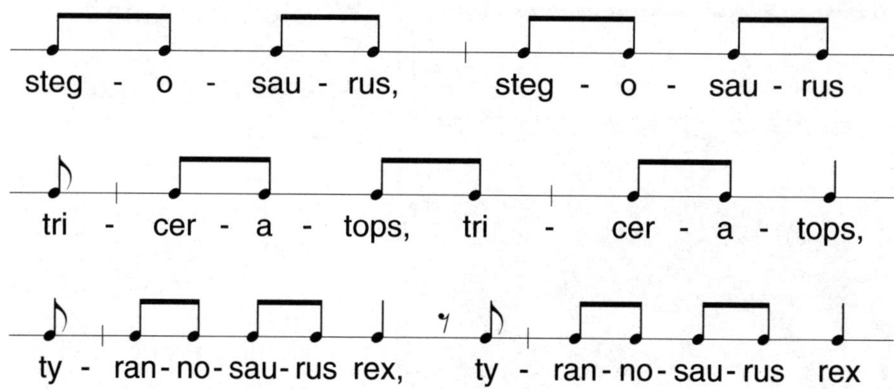

Description

Say the name of each dinosaur rhythmically, and then repeat the name several times while clapping each syllable. Ask the children to suggest additional dinosaur names to clap.

Child's Level

This activity is most appropriate for older preschool or kindergarten children who have some understanding of dinosaurs.

Why Appropriate

Young children are fascinated with the sounds of dinosaur names. Clapping the syllables emphasizes the rhythmic patterns of the language.

Modification

Once children are familiar with the names of dinosaurs and have had experience clapping the rhythms of these names, extend the activity by stringing several dinosaur names together. This increases the complexity of the activity.

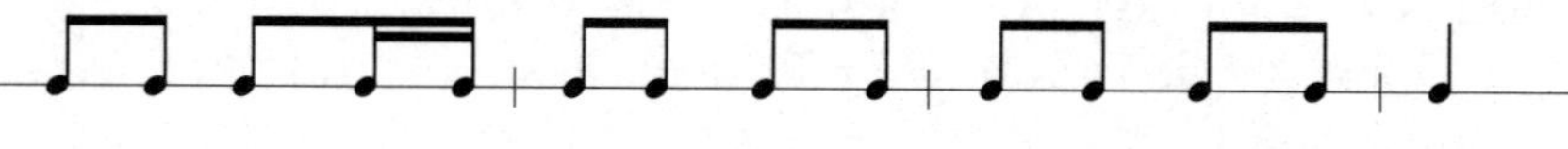

Musical Extension

After children have clapped the names of the dinosaurs, replace the claps with a rhythm instrument, such as drums.

Whole-Language Extension—Interactive Chart

Materials

- ▲ yellow poster board (or color desired), 20 by 22 inches
- ▲ green sentence strips (or color desired)
- ▲ dinosaur shapes cut from green construction paper

Description

Write the words "My favorite dinosaur is" on a sentence strip and mount it to the chart. Laminate the chart and the dinosaur shapes. Children can select their favorite dinosaur and hang it on the chart with magnetic tape, Velcro, or a paper fastener.

Integrated Curriculum Activities

Read dinosaur books, such as *Dinosaur, Dinosaur,* by Byron Barton, *Digging Up Dinosaurs,* by Aliki, and *Tyrannosaurus Was a Beast,* by Jack Prelutsky.

Put dinosaur word cards and dinosaur-shaped blank books in the writing center.

Add dinosaurs to the block area.

Examine fossils in the science area.

Assemble a collection of tiny dinosaurs for children to sort and classify by various attributes.

Graph children's favorite dinosaurs.

3.3 Friend

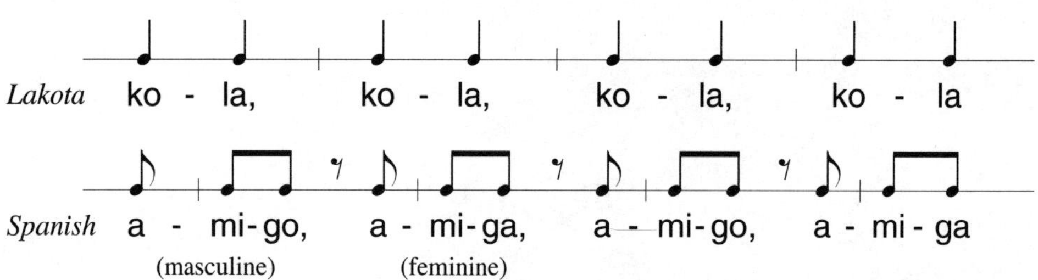

Description

Children can focus on the rhythm of other languages in this activity. Say the word *friend* several times in each language while clapping the syllables. Ask families or community representatives for additional words for *friend*.

Child's Level

This activity is appropriate for both preschool and kindergarten children.

Why Appropriate

Children are fascinated with learning words in other languages. Clapping the syllables emphasizes the rhythmic patterns of language.

Modification

Start with two or three words for *friend* and add additional ones over time.

Musical Extension

Once children are secure clapping the words for *friend,* they can substitute a rhythm instrument such as triangles for the claps.

Friend words in other languages:

Filipino kaibigan, pronounced *ki-be-gon*

French ami (masc.), amie (fem.)

German Freund ("eu" pronounced *"oy")*

Hindi pronounced *doast*

दोस्त

Indonesian teman, pronounced *tay-mon*

Japanese pronounced *tomodachi*

ともだち

Korean pronounced *chin gu*

친구

Urdu pronounced *doast*

Whole-Language Extension—Word Cards

Materials

- ▲ note cards
- ▲ markers

Description

Children are interested in hearing words in other languages and seeing how they look. Sometimes the notational systems are very different. Write the words for *friend* on note cards with the language they come from on the back. Laminate the cards and put them in the writing center for children to look at, copy, or discuss.

Integrated Curriculum Activities

Read books about friends, such as *My Friends,* by Taro Gomi, *My Best Friend,* by Pat Hutchins, and *What Is Your Language,* by Debra Leventhal.

Include pictures of friends from many cultures in your classroom.

Keep multicultural dolls, clothing, and cooking utensils in the dramatic play area.

3.4 Who Can Play?

Sally Moomaw
© 1980

(clap on beats)

|	|	|	|	
Who	can	play	*	with
Us	to-	day?	*	
(Jeffrey)	can	play	*	with
Us	to-	day.	*	

Description

Young children readily relate to activities that use their names. Encourage children to clap along on the beats as they say this chant, and include each child's name. This reinforces the idea that all of the children can participate with one another.

Child's Level

This chant is most appropriate for toddlers or young preschoolers.

Why Appropriate

The poem is short and easy to remember.
The beat is simple for even young children to feel.
Children are interested in the chant because their names are included.

Modifications

Try varying the rhythmic motions so that sometimes children pat their thighs on the beats instead of clapping.

This chant makes an excellent transitional tool. For example, if the class is about to go outside, change the word *today* to *outside* and call the children one at a time to move to the new location. (See chapter 7 for other examples of the use of music to facilitate transitions.)

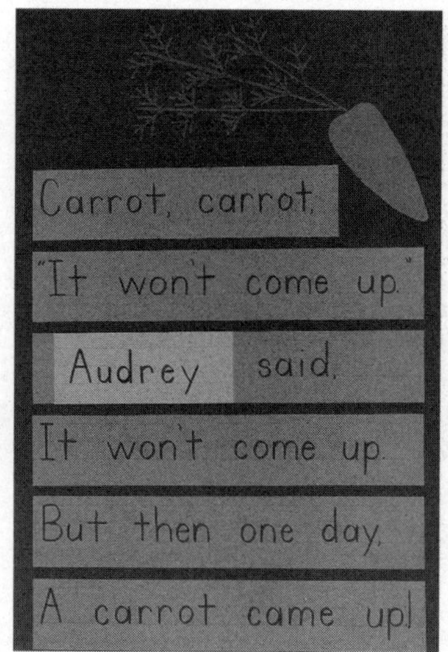

Musical Extension

Once children are very familiar with the chant and are accustomed to clapping the beats, substitute wood blocks for the clapping. This is an excellent early experience in using instruments.

Whole-Language Extension—Interactive Chart

Materials

- poster board, 22 by 17 inches
- sentence strips
- illustration of children playing

Description

Even very young preschoolers show interest in this chart. Print the words to the poem on sentence strips, but leave a blank space for the word *Jeffrey*. Mount the illustration and sentence strips to the board. Write each child's name on its own piece of sentence strip and laminate both the chart and name cards. Children can add their own names or their friends' names to the chart by hanging the word cards on a paper fastener.

Integrated Curriculum Activities

Make a class attendance chart (see activity 3.1).

Clap children's names or play them on wood blocks (see activity 3.1).

Read books about children and their play activities, such as *Tickle Tickle,* by Helen Oxenbury, and *Me Too,* by Susan Winter.

Add small toy people, such as from a Duplo building blocks set, to the manipulative area.

3.5 Monkeys, Monkeys

Sally Moomaw
© 1986, 1996

(clap on beats)

I	I	I	I
Mon-	keys,	mon-	keys
In	the	tree,	*
Throw	your	red	hats
Down	to	me.	*

Description

Chant the poem rhythmically with the children while clapping the beats.

Child's Level

This chant is appropriate for either preschool or kindergarten children.

Why Appropriate

The poem is short and rhythmic.
The beat is easy to feel.
The poem coordinates with several popular children's books.

Modification

Increase the rhythmic complexity by alternating clapping and patting the lap on the beats instead of just clapping.

Musical Extension

Once the children are relatively secure with clapping the beats, substitute a rhythm instrument for the clapping. Wood blocks, triangles, or drums work well. Have all the children play the same type of instrument so that the rhythm does not become obliterated by the competing sounds of the instruments.

Whole-Language Extension–Interactive Chart

Materials

- poster board, 28 by 22 inches
- sentence strips
- monkey pictures or stickers to illustrate the chart
- black tempera paint for the tree

Description

Print the words to the chant on sentence strips, with one sentence strip for each line. Leave a blank space for the word *red* that is large enough to accommodate any color word you wish to have children add to the chart. Paint a large tree on the poster board. Mount the monkeys and sentence strips to the poster board with rubber cement. Write additional color words on the remaining pieces of sentence strip and laminate both the board and the word cards. Use a paper fastener, magnetic tape, or Velcro to adhere the interactive word cards to the chart.

Integrated Curriculum Activities

Read books about monkeys and books about hats, such as *Caps for Sale,* by Esphyr Slobodkina, *Curious George,* by Margret and H. A. Rey, *Aunt Flossie's Hats,* by Elizabeth Fitzgerald Howard, and *Hats, Hats, Hats,* by Ann Morris.

Add a collection of tiny hats for sorting and classifying to the manipulative area (see *More Than Counting,* by Sally Moomaw and Brenda Hieronymus, activity 3.4).

Graph the children's hats, perhaps by color one day and a different attribute on another day.

3.6 Dinosaurs, Dinosaurs

Betsy Frame
Used by permission

(stamp on beats)

left	*right*	*left*	*right*	*left*	*right*	*left*	*right*
I	I	I	I	I	I	I	I
Dino-	saurs,	dino-	saurs,	tramp- ing	all a-	round,	*
Dino-	saurs,	dino-	saurs, their	bones are	all we've	found.	*
Dino-	saurs,	dino-	saurs,	lived so	long a-	go,	*
Dino-	saur	fos- sils	tell us	all we'll	ev- er	know.	*

Description

Stamp feet on the beats (left, right, left, right) as you chant this poem.

Child's Level

This chant is appropriate for both preschool and kindergarten children.

Why Appropriate

The chant is short and repetitive.
The beat is easy to feel.
Children are interested in dinosaurs.

Modification

Children can extend the chant by adding the names of specific dinosaurs to replace the word *dinosaur*.

	I	I	I	I	I	I	I	I
Di-	met- ro-	don, di-	met- ro-	don,	tramp- ing	all a-	round,	*
Di-	met- ro-	don, di-	met- ro-	don, its	bones are	all we've	found.	*

Musical Extension

Let children make the sounds of tramping dinosaurs by playing drums on the beats once they have had experience clapping or stamping the beats.

Whole-Language Extension—Big Book

Materials

- 6 pieces of construction paper, 12 by 18 inches each
- sentence strips
- dinosaur illustrations (use magazine pictures or trace dinosaur templates)
- book binding (such as notebook rings, staples, or spiral binding)

Description

Copy the words to the chant onto sentence strips with one line of the chant per page. Mount the sentence strips and illustrations onto the construction paper. Six pieces of paper are enough for the words to the chant plus a front and back cover. Laminate the pages and bind the book. Point to the words as children chant the rhyme.

Integrated Curriculum Activities

Clap the names of dinosaurs (see activity 3.2).

Put dinosaur counters and sand in the sensory table. Children can fish them out with tongs or nets and sort the dinosaurs by color, size, or type.

Estimate how many dinosaur counters fit in a small, clear jar.

Add dinosaur stampers to the art area.

3.7 Pizza

Sally Moomaw
© 1996

(clap on beats)

|	|	|	|	
Pizza	is	yummy,	*	We
like	it a	lot,	*	
(Sara)	likes	(mushrooms)	best	
On	the	top.	*	

Description

Children always seem interested in pizza. For this chant the children can add their names and what they like best on pizza. Encourage children to clap along on the beats as they all repeat the chant.

Child's Level

This chant is appropriate for preschoolers because it is so short; however, kindergartners typically love pizza and tend to be more interested in what their peers like on pizza than preschoolers. Therefore, this chant also works well in kindergarten, particularly as an early rhythm experience.

Why Appropriate

The chant is short and easy to remember.
The beat is easy to feel.
Children are interested in the topic.

Modification

For older children or children who have had many experiences with rhythm, change the clapping pattern to a more complex one. For example, children might try a clap, pat, stamp, pat pattern. Expect some miscues as children (and teachers) concentrate on combining both the words and the rhythmic pattern.

clap	*pat*	*stamp*	*pat*		*clap*	*pat*	*stamp*	*pat*
Pizza	is	yummy,	*	We	like	it a	lot,	*

Musical Extension

Combine a speech ostinato with the chant. Have one group chant a repeated phrase, such as *yummy,* while the second group chants the rhyme. This gives children experience in combining two lines of rhythm.

Group 1	yum-	my,	yum-	my,	yum-	my,	yum-	my
add Group 2	Piz-	za is	yummy,	* We	like	it a	lot,	*
to Group 1	yum-	my,	yum-	my,	yum-	my,	yum-	my
Group 2	Sara	likes	mushrooms	best	on	the	top.	*
Group 1	yum-	my,	yum-	my,	yum-	my,	yum-	my

Whole-Language Extension–Interactive Chart

Materials

- ▲ orange poster board (or color desired), 22 by 17 inches
- ▲ yellow sentence strips (or color desired)
- ▲ pizza illustration

Description

Children can change the poem to include their names and what pizza toppings they like best. Write the words to the poem on sentence strips and mount them to the poster board. Leave a blank space for the child's name and the pizza topping. Use pieces of sentence strip to write the names of the children and a variety of pizza ingredients. Add a pizza illustration to the chart and laminate both the chart and the word cards. Attach an extra piece of laminating film to the chart to form a pocket for the children's names and the pizza toppings. Children can either use the word cards to complete the rhyme or write their names and favorite pizza toppings on slips of paper to add to the chart.

Integrated Curriculum Activities

Set up a pizza restaurant in the dramatic play area.

Read books about pizza, such as *Pizza Party,* by Grace Maccarone, and *The Lady with the Alligator Purse,* by Nadine Bernard Westcott.

Graph the class' favorite pizza toppings.

3.8 Lost Toys

Sally Moomaw
© 1996

(clap on beats)

I	I	I	I
Teddy	bear,	teddy	bear,
He	was	lost,	*
Teddy	bear	in	the
Laundry	was	tossed,	*
Li-	sa,	Li-	sa,
came	and	found,	*
Teddy	bear	back,	*
Safe	and	sound.	*

Sally Moomaw
© 1996

(clap on beats)

I	I	I	I
Dog-	gie,	dog-	gie,
She	was	lost,	*
Dog-	gie	on	the
Floor	was	tossed,	*
Lit-	tle	girl	woke
up	and	found	*
Dog-	gie	back,	*
Safe	and	sound.	*

Description

Most children have experienced losing a favorite toy, and several children's books describe this situation. The teddy bear poem was inspired by the book *A Pocket for Corduroy,* by Don Freeman, while the doggie poem relates to *The Quilt,* by Ann Jonas. Clap the beats with children as they chant the poems. Children can add their own favorite toys and names to either poem.

Child's Level

These chants are appropriate for either preschool or kindergarten children.

Why Appropriate

The chants provide a musical connection to children's literature. It is easy to feel the beat in these two chants.

Modification

Vary the clapping ostinato to make this activity more challenging. For example, try 2 claps followed by 2 pats.

clap	*clap*	*pat*	*pat*
Teddy	bear,	teddy	bear,

clap	*clap*	*pat*	*pat*
He	was	lost,	*

(and so on)

Musical Extension

Have the children play the beats on a set of the same type of rhythm instrument—perhaps finger cymbals.

Whole-Language Extension–Story Starter

Materials

- ▲ paper
- ▲ markers or colored pencils

Description

Let children write their own versions of the chant by including their own names, the toys they lost, and where they were lost (see the illustration for an example).

Integrated Curriculum Activities

Read other books about teddy bears or lost toys, such as *Golden Bear,* by Ruth Young, *Corduroy,* by Don Freeman, and *Where Can It Be?,* by Ann Jonas.

Make teddy bear grid or path games for the math area (see *More Than Counting,* by Sally Moomaw and Brenda Hieronymus, activities 4.7, 5.3, and 5.14).

Put word cards of the class' favorite toys in the writing area.

Add teddy bear counters, fish nets, and small containers to the water table. Children can catch the bears and sort them by color or size if they choose.

3.9 Silly Sally Rap

Barton Canfield

clap	*pat*	*clap*	*pat*
/	/	/	/
Silly	up,	silly	down,
Sally	up,	Sally	down,
Silly	Sally	upside	down,
Sally's	silly	upside	down, and
Look, there's	(Jason)	upside	down.

Description

Alternate hand clapping and patting the lap on the beats as you recite this chant with the children.

Child's Level

This chant is most appropriate for older preschool or kindergarten children because of its longer length.

Why Appropriate

The beat is easy to feel.

The repetition of the text makes the chant easy to remember and fun to rap.

The chant relates to the popular children's book *Silly Sally,* by Audrey Wood.

Modification

If clapping and patting are at first too confusing for the children, just clap the beats until the children are more secure with the activity.

Musical Extension

Have children play wood blocks or rhythm sticks on the beats, as indicated by the slash marks on the chant.

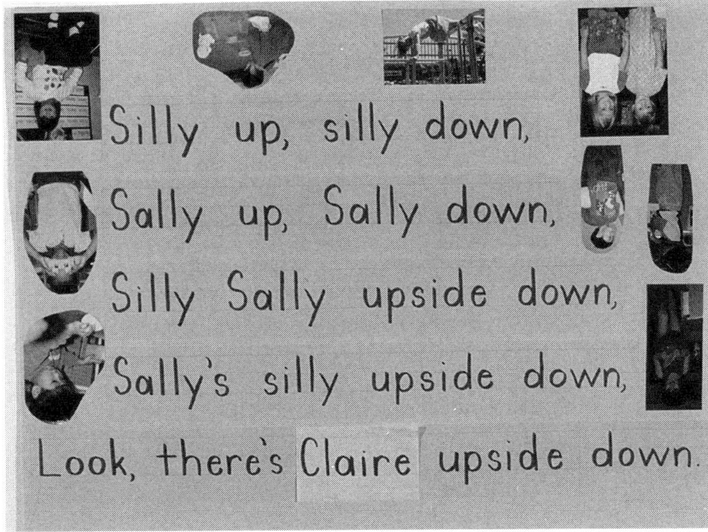

Whole-Language Extension—Interactive Chart

Materials

- ▲ yellow poster board (or color desired), 22 by 18 inches
- ▲ orange sentence strips (or color desired)
- ▲ photographs of all the children in the class

Description

Print the words to the chant on sentence strips, as illustrated. The interactive words are the names of the children in the class. They can add themselves or their friends to the "Silly Sally Rap." Illustrate the chart with photographs of the children in the class mounted upside down and laminate.

Integrated Curriculum Activities

Include the books *Silly Sally*, by Audrey Wood, *I Went Walking*, by Sue Williams, and *Rosie's Walk*, by Pat Hutchins, in the reading area.

Read the big book version of *Silly Sally* with the class.

Make handprints and footprints in the art area.

Place a container of sand and small novelty shoes in the science area so children can experiment with making footprints.

Add a collection of small shoes for sorting and classifying in the manipulative area (see *More Than Counting*, by Sally Moomaw and Brenda Hieronymus, activity 3.3).

3.10 5 Little Snowmen

Brenda Hieronymus
© 1986
Used by permission

(clap on beats)

I	I	I	I	I	I	I	I
5	little	snow-	men	standing	in a	row,	*
1,	2,	3,	4,	5	they	go,	*
Out	came the	sun	and it	shone	all	day,	*
1	little	snow-	man	melted	a-	way.	*
4	little	snow-	men	standing	in a	row,	*
1,	*	2,	3,	4	they	go,	*
Out	came the	sun	and it	shone	all	day,	*
1	little	snow-	man	melted	a-	way.	*
3	little	snow-	men	standing	in a	row,	*
1,	*	2,	*	3	they	go,	*
Out	came the	sun	and it	shone	all	day,	*
1	little	snow-	man	melted	a-	way.	*
2	little	snow-	men	standing	in a	row,	*
1,	*	*	*	2	they	go,	*
Out	came the	sun	and it	shone	all	day,	*
1	little	snow-	man	melted	a-	way.	*
1	little	snow-	man	standing	all a-	lone,	*
But	the	sun	no	long-	er	shone,	*
Out	came the	chil-	dren and	they	built	four,	*
5	little	snow-	men to-	gether	once	more.	*

Description
Clap the beats as you recite this chant with the children.

Child's Level
This chant is appropriate for both preschool and kindergarten children.

Why Appropriate
The beat is easy to feel.
The words repeat.
Children are interested in the text.

Modification

For younger children, use fewer snowmen—perhaps three. For very young children, use just one verse and say, "5 little snowmen melted away," for the last line.

Musical Extension

Have the children play the same type of rhythm instrument on the beats once they have had experience clapping. Triangles seem to go well with the idea of melting.

Whole-Math Extension—Snowmen Finger Puppets

Materials

- ▲ white and colored felt

Description

The finger puppets make a great math manipulative. Children are aided in constructing the relationship of subtracting by one when they can physically remove one snowman for each verse in this rhyme and visualize the result. Cut snowmen shapes from the white felt and whipstitch around the edges. Leave the bottoms open for fingers. Cut hats and faces from the colored felt and glue or sew them to the snowmen.

Integrated Curriculum Activities

Read books about snow, such as *The Snowy Day,* by Ezra Jack Keats, and for older children, *The Black Snowman,* by Phil Mendez.

Put snow in the sensory table so children can explore what happens to snow when it's brought inside.

Make snow-inspired artwork by blowing or brushing white paint across dark construction paper.

Let children dramatize the poem.

3.11 Our Garden

Sally Moomaw
© 1980, 1996

clap	*pat*	*clap*	*pat*	*clap*	*pat*	*clap*	*pat*
|	|	|	|	|	|	|	|
Let's	plant a	gar-	den and	watch	it	grow.	*
What	should we	do?	*	Do	you	know?	*
Plant	*	some	*	seeds,	*	*	*
Pull	up	all	the	weeds,	*	*	*
Watch	the	sun	shine,	wait	for	show-	ers,
Then	we can	look	at	all	the	flow-	ers.

Description
Children can alternate a clap and pat pattern on the beats as they chant this poem.

Child's Level
This chant is most appropriate for older preschool or kindergarten children because of its longer length.

Why Appropriate
The beat is easy to feel.

The subject coordinates well with planting activities, which are often a part of early childhood curriculum.

Modification
If alternating clapping and patting is too confusing for the children, backtrack to just clapping the beats until they are more secure with the rhythm.

Musical Extension
Children can play the beats on a rhythm instrument, such as wood blocks, to replace the claps and pats.

Whole-Language Extension—Big Book

Materials

- ▲ 12 pieces of white construction paper, 12 by 18 inches each
- ▲ photographs of the children gardening
- ▲ book binding (such as notebook rings or a spiral binder)

Description

Print the words to the chant on sentence strips. Lines one, two, five, and six take two pieces of paper each, while lines three and four are each one page in length. Use photographs of your class planting to illustrate the book. Laminate the pages and bind together.

Integrated Curriculum Activities

Plant a variety of types of seeds with your class.

Put mulch, buckets, shovels, and plastic flowers in the sensory table.

Change the dramatic play area into a flower shop with silk or plastic flowers, plastic flower pots, and price tags.

Put several sizes of clay flower pots in the music area (see activity 5.11).

Read books about flowers and planting, such as *Flower Garden,* by Eve Bunting, *The Lotus Seed,* by Sherry Garland, and *Pumpkin Pumpkin,* by Jeanne Titherington.

3.12 Carrot, Carrot

Sally Moomaw

(clap on beats)

<table>
<tr><td></td><td>|</td><td>|</td><td>|</td><td>|</td><td></td><td>|</td><td>|</td><td>|</td><td>|</td></tr>
<tr><td></td><td>Car-</td><td>rot,</td><td>car-</td><td>rot,</td><td>It</td><td>won't</td><td>come</td><td>up!</td><td>*</td></tr>
<tr><td></td><td>Planted</td><td>my</td><td>seed,</td><td>but</td><td>It</td><td>won't</td><td>come</td><td>up!</td><td>*</td></tr>
<tr><td></td><td>Watered</td><td>the</td><td>ground,</td><td>but</td><td>It</td><td>won't</td><td>come</td><td>up!</td><td>*</td></tr>
<tr><td></td><td>Sun</td><td>shone</td><td>down,</td><td>but</td><td>It</td><td>won't</td><td>come</td><td>up!</td><td>*</td></tr>
<tr><td></td><td>Pulled</td><td>the</td><td>weeds,</td><td>but</td><td>It</td><td>won't</td><td>come</td><td>up!</td><td>*</td></tr>
<tr><td></td><td>Moth-</td><td>er</td><td>said,</td><td>*</td><td>It</td><td>won't</td><td>come</td><td>up!</td><td>*</td></tr>
<tr><td></td><td>Fath-</td><td>er</td><td>said,</td><td>*</td><td>It</td><td>won't</td><td>come</td><td>up!</td><td>*</td></tr>
<tr><td></td><td>Broth-</td><td>er</td><td>said,</td><td>*</td><td>It</td><td>won't</td><td>come</td><td>up!</td><td>*</td></tr>
<tr><td></td><td>Sis-</td><td>ter</td><td>said,</td><td>*</td><td>It</td><td>won't</td><td>come</td><td>up!</td><td>*</td></tr>
<tr><td></td><td>Teach-</td><td>er</td><td>said,</td><td>*</td><td>It</td><td>won't</td><td>come</td><td>up!</td><td>*</td></tr>
<tr><td>But</td><td>then</td><td>one</td><td>day,</td><td>*</td><td></td><td>Yeah!</td><td>*</td><td>Yeah!</td><td>*</td></tr>
<tr><td>My</td><td>carrot</td><td>came</td><td>up!</td><td>*</td><td></td><td>Yeah!</td><td>*</td><td>Yeah!</td><td>*</td></tr>
<tr><td>My</td><td>carrot</td><td>*</td><td>came</td><td>*</td><td></td><td>up!</td><td>*</td><td>*</td><td>*</td></tr>
</table>

Description

This rhythm activity is a call and response. The leader says the words in regular print, and the children chant the italicized response. The chant correlates with the popular children's book *The Carrot Seed,* by Ruth Krauss.

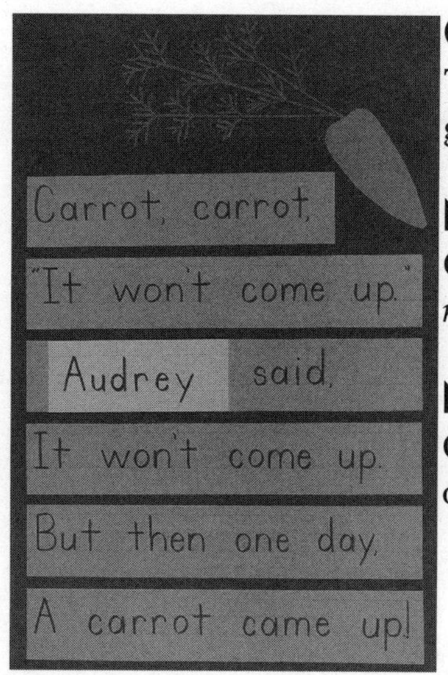

Child's Level

This chant is most appropriate for older preschool and kindergarten children because of its longer length.

Modification

Children can add additional words to the chant, such as *grandma* or *uncle*.

Musical Extension

Children can play a rhythm instrument, such as wood blocks, on the words "It won't come up!"

Whole-Language Extension–Interactive Chart

Materials

- ▲ brown poster board (or color desired), 28 by 20 inches
- ▲ sentence strips
- ▲ illustration of a carrot

Description

This chart uses just six lines of the chant so that children are not overwhelmed by the print. Print the words on sentence strips and mount them to the poster board, as shown. Use the carrot picture to illustrate the chart. Children can hang word cards with their own names or a friend's name on the chart after it has been laminated.

Integrated Curriculum Activities

Read books about planting vegetables, such as *Growing Vegetable Soup* and *Eating the Alphabet*, both by Lois Ehlert.

Cook with carrots and other vegetables. Vegetable soup is easy and fun.

Plan a variety of planting experiences for your class.

3.13 Pizza Combo

	I	I	I	I	I	I	I	I
Group 1	mush-	rooms	mush-	rooms	mush-	rooms	mush-	rooms
	I	𝄽	I	𝄽	I	𝄽	I	𝄽
Add Group 2	cheese	*	cheese	*	cheese	*	cheese	*
to Group 1	mush-	rooms	mush-	rooms	mush-	rooms	mush-	rooms
	⊓	⊓	⊓	⊓	⊓	⊓	⊓	⊓
Add Group 3	pep- per-	on- i	pep- per-	on- i	pep- per-	on- i	pep- per-	on- i
to Group 2	cheese	*	cheese	*	cheese	*	cheese	*
and Group 1	mush-	rooms	mush-	rooms	mush-	rooms	mush-	rooms

Description

Children combine the rhythms of three speech patterns in this more complex rhythm activity. Start by having the first group chant and clap *mush-rooms*. This is the steady beat. Add group 2 chanting and clapping the word *cheese*. Their claps are only half as fast as group 1. Then add group 3 chanting and clapping *pep-per-on-i*. This group claps twice as fast as the *mush-room* group. This activity gives children a chance to experience an ensemble situation where they are performing one line of music but simultaneously hearing two other lines.

Child's Level

This activity is most appropriate for older preschool or kindergarten children who have had substantial experience with rhythm activities.

Why Appropriate

The words are familiar to most children.
Children are interested in words related to pizza.

Modification

You may wish to start with just two groups until the children are comfortable performing two lines of rhythm together.

Musical Extension

Once children are accustomed to clapping the words, each group can be given a specific type of instrument to play in place of the claps. For example, group 1 might play wood blocks, group 2 triangles, and group 3 maracas. Using a different instrument for each line of music helps children auditorily distinguish each line. However, if diverse instruments are combined on the same line of music, the rhythm becomes difficult to determine.

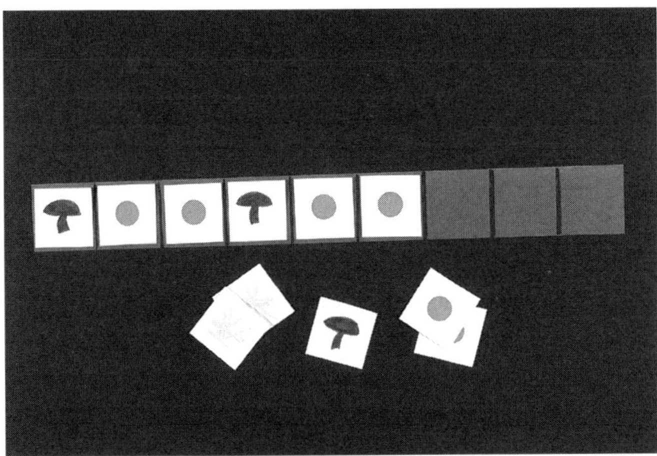

Whole-Math Extension

Materials

- ▲ stickers or cut-outs of mushrooms, pepperoni, and cheese
- ▲ poster board strip, 2 by 18 inches

Description

Mark off 2-inch squares along the poster board. Children can use the pizza topping cut-outs to experiment with patterning. Once they have formed a pattern, encourage them to chant the pattern. This helps some children construct the idea of a pattern and also perceive patterns in music and language. For example:

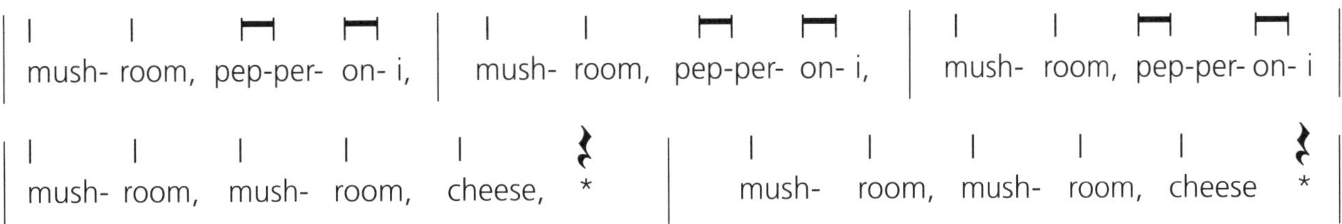

Integrated Curriculum Activities

Make pretend pizzas and toppings out of poster board and put them in the dramatic play area.

Put pizza word cards in the writing center.

Make pizza with the children.

3.14 Rain Sounds

	|	|	|	|	|	|	|	|
Group 1	drip	drop	drip	drop	drip	drop	drip	drop
	┌┐	┌┐	┌┐	┌┐	┌┐	┌┐	┌┐	┌┐
Add Group 2	pit- ter	pat- ter	pit- ter	pat- ter	pit- ter	pat- ter	pit- ter	pat- ter
to Group 1	drip	drop	drip	drop	drip	drop	drip	drop
	|	𝄽	|	𝄽	|	𝄽	|	𝄽
Add Group 3	splash	*	splash	*	splash	*	splash	*
to Group 2	pit- ter	pat- ter	pit- ter	pat- ter	pit- ter	pat- ter	pit- ter	pat- ter
and Group 1	drip	drop	drip	drop	drip	drop	drip	drop

Description

In this activity, children combine the different rhythms of three rain sounds. The first group begins by chanting and clapping *drip drop*. This provides the steady beat. Group 2 joins in on cue with the words and clapping for *pitter patter* at twice the speed of group 1. Finally group 3 is added with the word *splash*. This group claps only half as fast as the first group. (The alignment of the three lines can be seen in the graph above.) This activity gives children the experience of performing one line of music while listening to two different lines.

Child's Level

This activity is most appropriate for older preschool and kindergarten children who have had substantial experience with rhythm activities.

Why Appropriate

Children are familiar with the words associated with rain sounds. The rhythmic patterns of the words are clear.

Modification

You may wish to start with just two groups until the children are comfortable performing two lines of rhythm together.

Musical Extension

Once the children are accustomed to clapping the words, each group can be given a specific type of instrument to play in place of the claps. For example, group 1 might play wood blocks, group 2 bells, and group 3 cymbals for the *splash.*

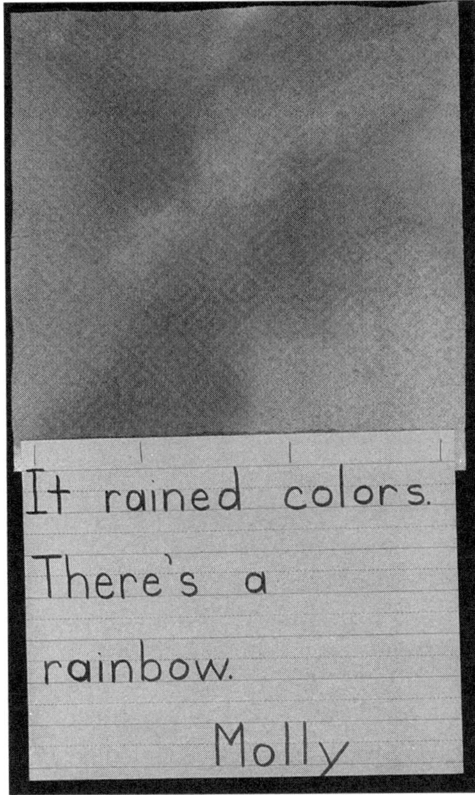

Whole-Language Extension–Story Dictation/Eyedropper Painting

Materials

- ▲ white paper towels or coffee filters
- ▲ eyedroppers
- ▲ water colored with food coloring
- ▲ lined paper

Description

Children can make raindrop pictures by using eyedroppers and colored water on the paper towels or coffee filters. Take dictation as the children describe or tell stories about their pictures. Older children may wish to do their own writing. After the pictures have dried, display them with the stories.

Integrated Curriculum Activities

Read books about rain, such as *Umbrella,* by Taro Yashima, and *The Napping House,* by Audrey Wood.

Ask parents for donations of umbrellas and take a walk in the rain, as long as there is no lightning.

Put rainsticks in the music area (activity 5.6).

Sing rain songs, such as "Thunder" (activity 2.10).

3.15 Rain, Rain, Go Away

Group 1	drip	drop	drip	drop	drip	drop	drip	drop
Add Group 2 **to** Group 1	pit - ter drip	pat - ter drop	pit - ter drip	pat - ter drop	pit - ter drip	pat - ter drop	pit - ter drip	pat - ter drop
Add Group 3 **to** Group 2 **and** Group 1	splash pit - ter drip	* pat - ter drop	splash pit - ter drip	* pat - ter drop	splash pit - ter drip	* pat - ter drop	splash pit - ter drip	* pat - ter drop
Add Group 4 **to** Group 3 **and** Group 2 **and** Group 1	**Rain,** splash pit - ter drip	**rain,** * pat - ter drop	**go a-** splash pit - ter drip	**way,** * pat - ter drop	**Come a-** splash pit - ter drip	**gain some** * pat - ter drop	**oth - er** splash pit - ter drip	**day,** * pat - ter drop
Group 4 Group 3 Group 2 Group 1	**We want** splash pit - ter drip	**to go** * pat - ter drop	**out and** splash pit - ter drip	**play !** * pat - ter drop				

Description

The three rhythmic ostinati from activity 3.14 are now combined with the familiar chant "Rain, Rain, Go Away." This creates a four-part piece for children to perform. Compositions such as this are often called *Orffstrations* after the German composer and music educator Carl Orff (1895–1982), who developed the style.

Child's Level

This activity is most appropriate for kindergarten children who have had many experiences with rhythm activities.

Why Appropriate

The chant is clear and simple.
It is easy to feel the beat.
The rain sounds coordinate with the chant.

Modification

You can make this activity much easier by starting with just one line of rain sounds, such as *drip drop,* to accompany the chant.

Musical Extension

Once the children are secure with chanting and clapping the words, groups 1, 2, and 3 can be given a specific type of instrument to substitute for the claps, as in activity 3.14. Group 4 supplies the chant.

Whole-Language Extension–Interactive Chart

Materials

- ▲ royal blue poster board, 25 by 22 inches
- ▲ light blue sentence strips
- ▲ umbrellas cut from colorful construction paper or wallpaper

Description

Alter the words to the chant slightly so that children can put their own names and the names of other children into the poem. Print the words to the chant on sentence strips as shown, but leave room for two names to be inserted. Mount the sentence strips and umbrellas to the chart with rubber cement and laminate. Add paper fasteners or magnetic tape to the chart so children can hang the name cards.

Integrated Curriculum Activities

Sing rain songs, such as "Thunder" (activity 2.10).

Make a math grid game using cloud stickers for the board and clear marble chips for the counters (see *More Than Counting,* by Sally Moomaw and Brenda Hieronymus, chapter 4).

Include books about rain, such as *Rain,* by Peter Spier, in the book area.

Instruments

On a rainy day the teacher decided to use rhythm sticks at group time so the children could imitate the sound of the rain. Each child had a pair of sticks, one of which was grooved. The children soon discovered that they could either tap the sticks together or scrape them to create different sounds. The children played the rhythm sticks to accompany a rain song. Suddenly Tony announced that he had discovered how to make both sounds at once. By using a circular motion with his top stick as he hit the sticks together, he could make both a tapping and a scraping sound on the same stroke.

▲ ▲ ▲

Instruments offer children another way to explore and construct the world of music. Children become excited when they see instruments and are eager to begin producing sounds. Teachers, on the other hand, sometimes feel a headache coming on at the mere thought of handing out instruments to groups of eager children. This chapter explores systematic and manageable ways to plan and implement group experiences with instruments.

Teachers' Questions

Why is it important to include instruments in the curriculum?

Using instruments opens a whole new dimension in the understanding of sound and the awareness of music in young children. Through experimenting with instruments, children construct important concepts about the nature of sound and how the instrument and the way it is played affect sound. Listening to instruments sharpens children's auditory skills. Instruments also provide children with a means for expressing their feelings and creativity. Playing musical instruments helps children develop their eye-hand coordination and fine motor skills.

What types of instruments are appropriate to use with young children?

Three types of instruments may be used successfully with young children: rhythm instruments, melody instruments, and accompanying instruments. Rhythm instruments are those that produce a variety of nonpitched sounds when struck or scraped. Wood blocks, triangles, and drums are examples. Melody instruments produce sounds with specific pitches so that tunes can be played on them. Xylophones, pianos, and electronic keyboards are melodic instruments. Accompanying instruments produce several tones simultaneously, thus creating chords that can be used to accompany melodies. The autoharp (discussed in chapter 2) is an example of an accompanying instrument.

What kinds of activities involving instruments should teachers plan?

Teachers should plan for both group time use of instruments and individual exploration of instruments in music centers. Playing instruments in groups gives children the opportunity to experience the communal creation of music. Individual experimentation with instruments is also very valuable because it allows children more unlimited time to construct knowledge about sound and music and to create. The activities in this chapter are designed for groups of children. You'll find ideas for using instruments in classroom music centers in chapter 5.

How are instruments used in groups?

Children use instruments to play rhythmic patterns in speech, emphasize the beat in chants and songs, and add specific tone color to songs. Teachers can use instruments in listening games that heighten children's auditory discrimination skills.

How should teachers introduce instruments?

Teachers should introduce instruments one at a time so that children can learn the sounds and characteristics of each one. The teacher should begin by giving the children one type of instrument for the first several sessions. When the children clearly recognize the sound this instrument makes, the teacher can introduce a second type of instrument. More instruments can be added gradually, but always one type of instrument at a time. Meanwhile, the teacher can continue reviewing with the children the instruments they have already played so that they remember the individual sound of each instrument.

What sequence should teachers follow as they introduce children to rhythm instruments?

The introduction of rhythm instruments might follow a pattern of free exploration followed by several days of specific activities involving the instruments. Plan listening games to review the instruments once the children have had experience with more than one.

The teacher might choose to start with wood blocks, as in activity 4.1. On the first day, the teacher can play a wood block while the children listen. After the group has discussed the characteristics of the wood block, such as the material it is made of and its sound, the teacher can hand out several wood blocks and invite the children to play them. Once every child has had a turn, the teacher can collect the wood blocks.

On the second day, the children can begin to use the wood blocks to create music. The teacher might start by having them clap the rhythms of their names (activity 3.1). The teacher can then distribute the wood blocks and the children can play the names on them. Since the motion of playing a wood block is very similar to clapping, making the transfer is usually easy for children. Since they have just clapped the same activity, they know what to do with the wood blocks when they get them and management problems are greatly reduced. Once the activity is finished, the teacher can again collect the wood blocks before continuing with her group time plans.

After the children have had the opportunity to play the wood blocks for several days, the teacher can introduce a contrasting instrument, such as a triangle, and follow the same procedure. New instruments are introduced in this fashion as the year progresses. Children can compare and contrast the sounds of the instruments they know through music listening games, such as activity 4.15.

What should teachers avoid when using instruments with children?

Teachers should avoid having children play a variety of instruments simultaneously—the so-called rhythm band method. When children play many different instruments together, noise rather than music is generally the result. Children are unable to distinguish the sounds of any particular instrument or hear the music. It is also difficult for them to focus on the rhythm and feel the beat.

What guidelines should teachers follow in order to avoid management problems when using instruments with groups?

Distribute the instruments for only a specific segment of group time, and practice the activity first by clapping. The temptation to play with the instruments is too great for many young children to resist. This problem is averted when the teacher collects the instruments immediately following their use. In addition, if the children first practice an activity by clapping, they have a good idea of how to use the instruments once they are distributed. This eliminates much of the rowdiness that can occur when children do not understand the function of the instruments.

What are the first instruments schools should purchase when building a music program?

A good starting point is to acquire sets of two contrasting rhythm instruments. Wood blocks and triangles are good choices. Both are relatively inexpensive, so schools can often purchase enough sets for children to play them in groups. Wood blocks have a pleasant, resonant sound. Some types are serrated, or grooved, so that they can be tapped or scraped, thus making them two instruments in one. Since triangles are metallic, they make a very different sound from wood blocks and allow children to compare an instrument made of metal with one made of wood. Schools should consider purchasing one wood block and one triangle that are a different size from the rest. Then children can compare the effect that size has on pitch (see chapter 5 for ideas).

Schools should also consider investing in a quality xylophone or glockenspiel. (Glockenspiels are similar to xylophones but have metal bars.) This gives children the opportunity to create melodies or re-create tunes they have heard. The autoharp is an ideal accompanying instrument for schools to purchase.

How many instruments of each type are needed?

It is ideal, but not necessary, to have enough of each type of rhythm instrument for the entire class, especially in preschool. Young children have a hard time waiting for something as intriguing as an instrument. They can usually be patient for short amounts of time, though, as long as they are assured that they will get a turn in just a few minutes. Therefore, teachers need enough of each type of instrument for at least one-third to one-half of the class. Activities can be repeated two or three times so that everyone gets to play an instrument during any given group time. Waiting until tomorrow can seem like an eternity for a three year old.

Can teachers make instruments?

Yes! There are many instruments that teachers can make inexpensively to augment their classroom instrument collections. Quality of sound is an important criterion in an instrument whether it is purchased or teacher-made. You'll find many examples of quality, teacher-made instruments in this chapter and in chapter 5.

Can children play melody instruments together?

Older preschool children and especially kindergarten children can combine the playing of Orff-style xylophones and glockenspiels. These instruments have removable bars so teachers can remove any bars the children do not need. See activities 4.12, 4.13, and 4.14 for ideas on combining melody instruments.

What criteria should teachers follow when purchasing instruments?

The quality of sound and durability of the instrument are both important. Just as teachers select quality, long-lasting furniture for a dramatic play area, so should they select well-made, durable musical instruments. If children are to become discriminating listeners, they need the opportunity to hear and play resonant instruments. Avoid instruments made of plastic or ones included in toy rhythm band sets. Manufacturers often identify the best-quality melody and percussion instruments as being for use with the Orff method. Look for high-quality xylophones and glockenspiels with wooden frames, an assortment of sizes, and removable bars.

What are some special considerations when using instruments with inclusion children?

It is important to use high-quality, resonant instruments with children who have hearing impairments. Modify instruments for children with orthopedic disabilities.

Most children who are hearing impaired have some residual hearing. They have a much better chance of hearing, at least in part, a high-quality instrument than an inexpensive one because quality instruments are more resonant. This means the instruments have a wider range of vibration. Children who are hearing impaired may hear some part of that vibrating spectrum.

For children who have use of only one hand or one side of the body, instruments such as triangles can be suspended from a rack (see activities in this chapter). Other instruments can be set on the ground. For example, a rectangular wood block, as opposed to a cylindrical one, can rest on the ground while the child plays it. Encourage children who are visually impaired to not only listen to the sounds of instruments but also feel the vibrations.

Instrument Activities

4.1 Wood Blocks

Description

Wood blocks, or *tone blocks* as they are sometimes called, are hollow wooden cylinders or rectangular-shaped blocks that produce a resonant tone when struck by a wooden beater. Some wood blocks have grooves carved into them so they can also be scraped. Wood blocks are an ideal instrument for playing rhythms since they produce one clear sound each time they are struck. They are also relatively inexpensive.

Suggested Activity—Zoo Animal Rhythms

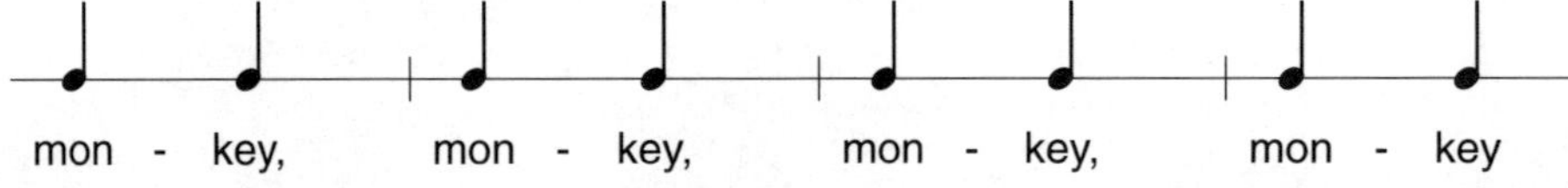

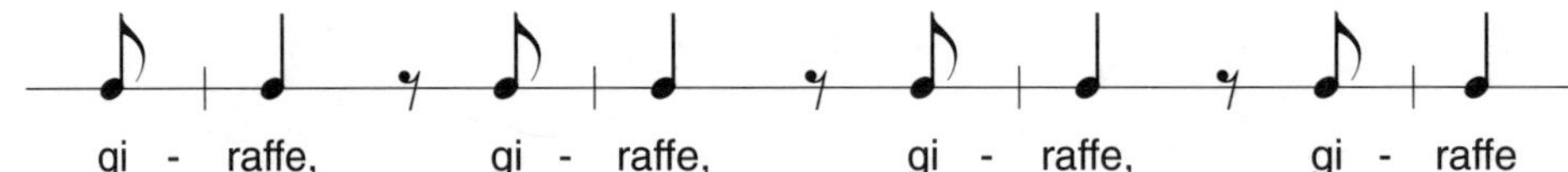

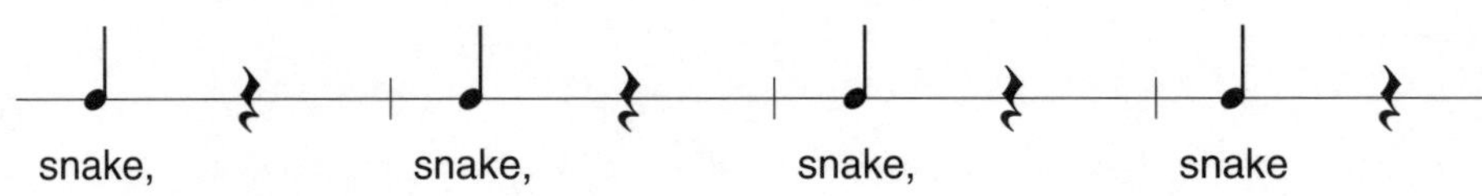

Description

This is a good beginning activity for introducing instruments. Have the children clap the names of the animals. Then distribute the wood blocks and substitute playing the animal names for clapping them. Children can add additional zoo animals to the activity. Since there is no singing involved, children can focus on the rhythm of the words and the sound of the wood blocks.

Child's Level

This activity is appropriate for either preschool or kindergarten children.

Suggestions for Additional Activities

Play wood blocks on other speech pattern activities (see activities 3.1, 3.2, and 3.3).

Use wood blocks to play the beats of chants (see activities 3.5 and 3.9).

Add wood blocks to a song for tone color. For example, try playing the letters of each child's name in "Bingo, Revisited" (activity 2.11) after the children have had experience clapping them.

Put two sizes of wood blocks in the music center (activity 5.1) so that children can experiment with how size affects pitch.

4.2 Triangles

Description

Triangles are metal rods bent into a triangular shape and played with a metal striker. In order to sound properly, the triangle must be suspended from a triangle holder. A string or pipe cleaner will also serve this purpose. Triangles produce a lovely, ringing sound that contrasts nicely with the sound of the wood block (activity 2.1).

Suggested Activity–Ice Cream Truck

Description

Children can use triangles to produce the "dings" of the ice cream truck and thus add tone color to the song. Start by clapping just on the word *ding* as you sing the song with the children. Then substitute triangles for the claps. Children can add their own names and their favorite ice cream flavors to the song.

Child's Level

This activity is appropriate for either preschool or kindergarten children.

Suggestions for Additional Activities

Play triangles on speech patterns (see activities 3.1, 3.2, and 3.3).

Use triangles to play the beats of chants (see activities 3.4, 3.8, and 3.9).

Accompany a song by playing triangles on the beats. Activities 2.3 and 2.6 lend themselves well to the tone color of the triangle.

Put two sizes of triangles in the music center (activity 5.3) so that children can experiment with how size affects pitch.

4.3 Corn Maracas

Description

Maracas are typically dried gourds or hollow wooden disks filled with beans or seeds. They produce a rattling sound when shaken. To create the corn maracas used in this activity, fill clear plastic bottles, about 7 inches tall, with dried kernels of multicolored corn. Glue or tape the tops shut. The children can see what is making the sound since the bottles are clear, and the colored corn is attractive.

Suggested Activity–Shiver, Brrr

Sally Moomaw

Dmin Dmin
Oo - oo, oo - oo, shi- ver, shi- ver, shi- ver, shi- ver, brrr!

Dmin Dmin
Oo - oo, oo - oo, shi- ver, shi- ver, shi- ver, shi- ver, brrr! I'll

A7
zip my coat up and keep it closed, So
put my hat on to keep me warm, So
pull my mittens on — over my hands When the

A7
I don't freeze when the cold wind blows,
I don't freeze in the wind - y storm,
winter wind blows — a - cross the land,

Dmin Dmin
Oo - oo, oo - oo, shi- ver, shi- ver, shi- ver, shi- ver, brrr!

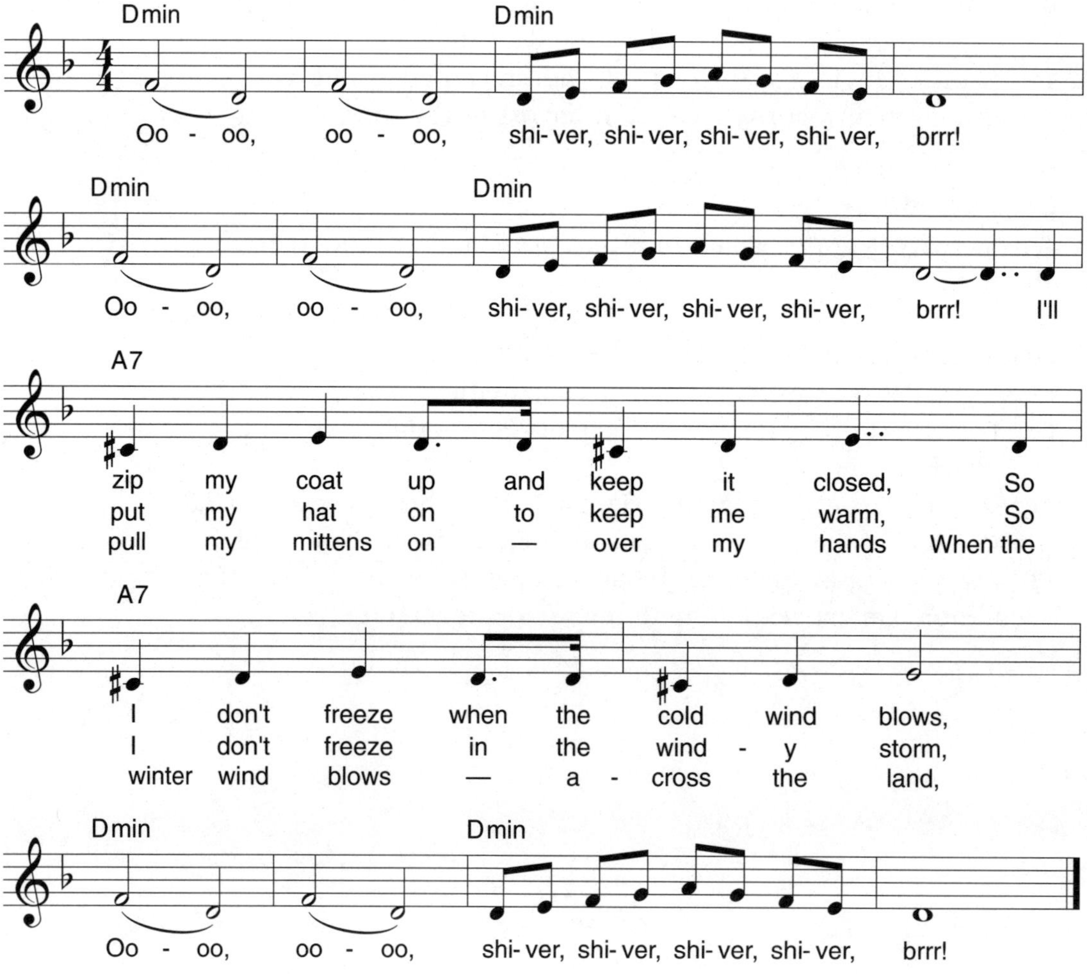

Description

Children like to sing this song and hug themselves during the *shiver* parts. The corn maracas add tone color to the song. Children can use them just on the words *shiver* and *brrr* to create a sound similar to the wind blowing through tree branches or dried weeds and grass.

Child's Level

This activity is appropriate for either preschool or kindergarten children.

Suggestions for Additional Activities

Add maracas to autumn songs such as activity 2.5.

Put maracas made from clear bottles or jars in the music area (activity 5.4). Use a variety of fillers so the children can explore how different materials affect the sound of the maracas.

4.4 Water Maracas

Description

Water maracas provide an interesting tone color for songs about sea animals, water, or rain. To create water maracas, fill clear plastic bottles, about 7 inches tall, with about 2 inches of water. Color the water blue with food coloring, if desired. Glue or tape the tops shut. As with the corn maracas, children can see what is creating the sound when they shake the clear bottles.

Suggested Activity–Swish, Swish, Swish

See activity 2.15 for the music and words of this song.

Description

The water maracas are perfect for creating the swishing sound of fish swimming through the water. Children can play the maracas on the beats as they sing the song.

Child's Level

This activity is appropriate for either preschool or kindergarten children.

Suggestions for Additional Activities

Explore other activities that involve the sound water makes, such as glissando cans (activity 5.9) and tuned water bottles (activity 5.15).

Use water maracas to accompany rain songs, such as activity 2.10.

Chant and clap the names of sea animals and then use water maracas to play those names.

4.5 Finger Cymbals

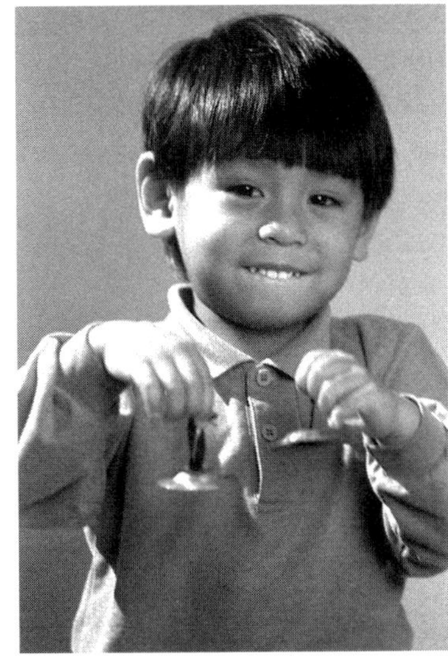

Description

Finger cymbals are small concave disks made of brass. They are played by holding one cymbal horizontal to the floor and tapping the edge with the other cymbal. Finger cymbals make a delicate, tinkling sound.

Suggested Activity—Snow Boy, Snow Girl

Description

Children can play finger cymbals on the beats of this song. The tinkling sound of the finger cymbals suits the words.

Sally Moomaw

Child's Level

This activity is most appropriate for preschoolers because of the song's short length. Kindergartners might enjoy playing finger cymbals on one of the longer activities listed below.

Suggestions for Additional Activities

Play finger cymbals on the beats of chants (see activities 3.8 and 3.10).

Use finger cymbals for one line of a multiline rhythm activity (see activity 3.14 or 3.15).

Add finger cymbals to a dance area (see activity 6.15).

4.6 Jingle Bells

Description

Jingle bells are small, round bells mounted on handles or bracelets. They are inexpensive to purchase. You can make them by sewing bells (found in craft stores) onto cloth ponytail holders or elastic straps.

Suggested Activity—Hear Our Jingle Bells

Sally Moomaw

Description

The jingle bells supply the tone color suggested by the words to the song.

Child's Level

This activity is most appropriate for toddlers or young preschoolers. Older children may wish to use jingle bells on some of the activities listed below.

Suggestions for Additional Activities

Use jingle bells for tone color (see activity 2.6).

Use jingle bells for one line of a multiline rhythm activity (see activities 3.13, 3.14, or 3.15).

Put several sizes of jingle bells in the music area so children can explore the effect that size has on pitch.

4.7 Scraped Shells

Description

Some types of seashells are concave in shape and have ridges. They make excellent scraping instruments.

Suggested Activity—Walking Slow!

The turtle walks so slowly,
On his back, a checkered dome.
How could he walk quickly
When he's carrying his home?

The snail walks so slowly,
He's as quiet as a mouse.
How could he walk quickly
When he's carrying his house?

The hermit crab walks so slowly,
A shell upon his back.
How could he walk quickly
When he's carrying a pack?

Sally Moomaw
© 1996

Description

After children have learned the words to this poem, they can emphasize the rhythm by scraping a pair of shells on each syllable. Since all of the animals in the poem have shells, using shells as instruments seems appropriate.

Child's Level

This activity is appropriate for kindergarten children. Younger children can use fewer verses.

Suggestions for Additional Activities

Clap the names of sea animals to feel the rhythm. Then substitute scraping the shells for the claps.

Use seashells to play the beats in songs such as "Swish, Swish, Swish" (activity 2.15).

Put serrated seashells of various sizes in the music area for further exploration.

4.8 Coconut Shells

Description

Hollowed-out coconut shells make resonant instruments and are often used to depict the sound of horses' hooves. To make your own, drill a hole in a coconut and drain the milk. Cut the shell in half and scrape out the coconut meat. Allow the shells to dry.

Involve the children in making this instrument, if possible, because they always seem to be curious about what is inside a coconut.

Play the shells with a wooden beater or tap them together.

Suggested Activity—Come Little Pony

Sally Moomaw
© 1997

I	I	I	I	I	I	I	I
Come	little	po-	ny,	Come	little	po-	ny,
Clip	clop,	clip	clop,	stop.	*	*	*
Come	little	po-	ny,	Come	little	po-	ny,
Clip	clop,	clip	clop,	stop.	*	*	*
When	I	give	him	oats	to	eat,	*
Danc-	ing,	danc-	ing	go	his	feet.	*
Go	little	po-	ny,	go	little	po-	ny,
Clip	clop,	clip	clop,	hop!	*	*	*

Description

Coconut shells are perfect for accompanying this chant because they sound like a pony's hooves. Clap the beats with the children as they learn the words, then add coconut shells on the words "clip clop, clip clop, stop (hop)."

Child's Level

This activity is most appropriate for older preschool or kindergarten children because of its longer length. Younger children can use coconut shells to accompany shorter activities.

Suggestions for Additional Activities

Play the names of farm animals on coconut shells.
Use coconut shells to play the beats in songs (see activity 6.8).
Put coconut shells in the music area for further exploration.

4.9 Cymbals

Description

Cymbals are concave brass disks with handles. They can be played in pairs or singly. When played as a pair, hold them parallel to each other and tilted slightly, with one slightly higher than the other. Use an arc-like motion to strike the bottom symbol with the top cymbal. To play a single cymbal, suspend it by the strap and strike it with a wooden beater. In this way, two children can play one pair of cymbals.

While some children's cymbals make an unpleasant sound, true brass cymbals have a resonant ring. It is worth paying more for quality children's cymbals since their aesthetically pleasing sound encourages children to regard them as musical instruments rather than noisemakers.

Suggested Activity—Thunder

See activity 2.10 for the music and words of this song.

Description

Cymbals are perfect for re-creating the sound of thunder. Children can start by clapping the uppercase words at the end of each line. Then they can substitute cymbals for the claps.

Child's Level

This activity is appropriate for either preschool or kindergarten children. Younger children can sing just the first verse.

Suggestions for Additional Activities

Use cymbals to make the *splash* sound in activity 3.14.

Suspend a cymbal in the music area from a hook or rack (see activity 5.3 for an example of a rack). Put out several types of mallets, such as beaters with wood, felt, and sponge heads, so that children can experiment with how the material of the beater affects the sound. Instructions for making these beaters can be found in activity 5.2.

4.10 Drums

Description

Drums are wooden cylinders with skin or plastic heads stretched over one or both ends. They can be played with either the hand or a beater. Drums should be played approximately midway between the center of the drum and the rim. When they are struck in the center of the drumhead, a dull "thunk" is produced.

Drums vary greatly in both quality and price. Latin drums are often better made and more resonant than inexpensive drums with handles. Orff-type drums with tunable heads are very resonant.

Suggested Activity–The Hippopotamus

See activity 6.7 for the music and words of this song.

Description

Drums are ideal for accompanying this song since they make a sound like the *thud* of the hippopotamus. Start by clapping the beats as you sing the song with the children, then substitute drums for the claps.

Child's Level

This song is appropriate for either preschool or kindergarten children.

Suggestions for Additional Activities

Use drums to play speech patterns (see activity 3.2).

Play the beats of chants on the drums. "Dinosaurs, Dinosaurs" (activity 3.6) is especially well suited for drums.

Put two sizes of drums in the music area so children can construct how the size of an instrument affects the pitch.

At another time, put a drum with several types of mallets, such as beaters with wood, felt, and sponge heads, in the music area. Children can explore how the type of beater affects the sound (see activity 5.2).

4.11 Tambourines

Description

Tambourines are small drums with metal disks mounted on the rim. The disks jingle together when the tambourine is struck or shaken.

Suggested Activity–It's So Good

Sally Moomaw

Description

Tambourines lend themselves well to the happy sound of this song. Children can play them on the beats or try a slightly more complex pattern such as the one included above.

Child's Level

This activity is appropriate for either preschool or kindergarten children. Use a simpler, steady-beat pattern of accompaniment for younger children.

Suggestions for Additional Activities

Use tambourines to highlight particular parts of songs, such as the *shivers* in activity 4.3.

Add tambourines to the dance area (activity 6.15).

4.12 It Was Snow (Ensemble)

Child's Level

This activity is most appropriate for preschool or kindergarten children who have had many experiences with rhythm activities.

Description

In this activity, the children accompany the song "It Was Snow" by playing ostinati (repeated melodic patterns) on Orff glockenspiels or xylophones. (See activity 5.14 for more information about these instruments.) The children should already be familiar with the song so that they can sing it easily. Performing and listening to melodic ostinati help children learn to distinguish the separate lines in a piece of music while still hearing the whole.

For an initial ensemble activity, the children could play a simple ostinato such as repeated Cs. Start by having one child play the steady beat ostinato. Then the group can join in singing the song as the ostinato continues.

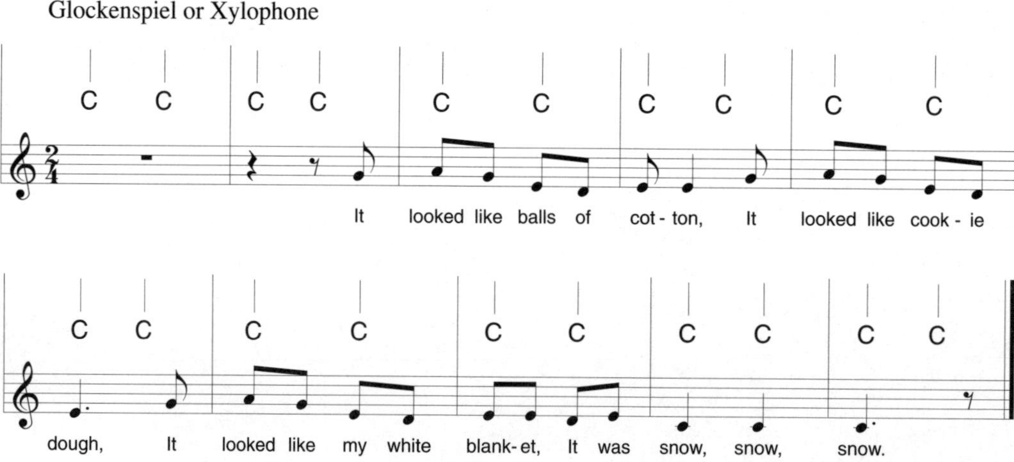

Later, introduce a second ostinato. Again, the child playing the beat begins, followed by the child playing the second ostinato, and finally by the singing.

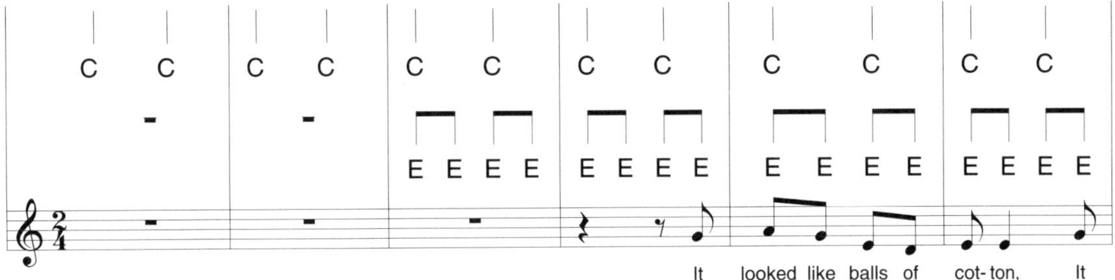

As the children become more advanced, add a third ostinato. As before, begin the song with the child playing the beat, followed by each successive ostinato, and finally by the singing.

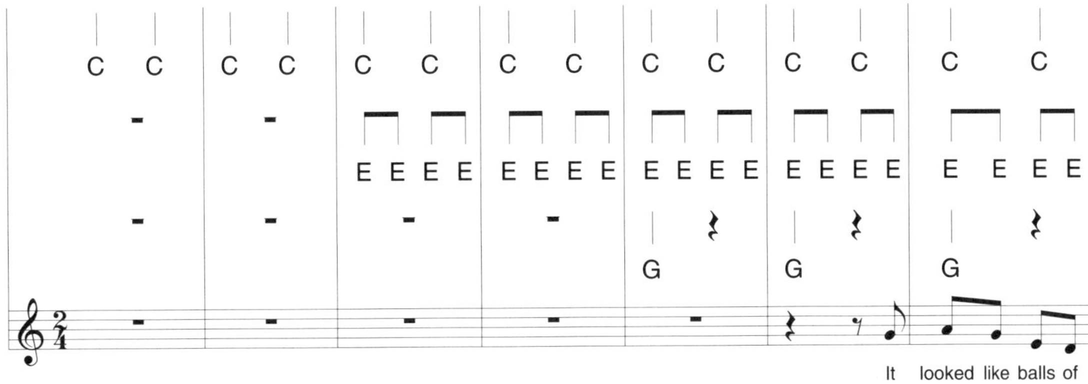

The following is a more complex three-ostinato arrangement.

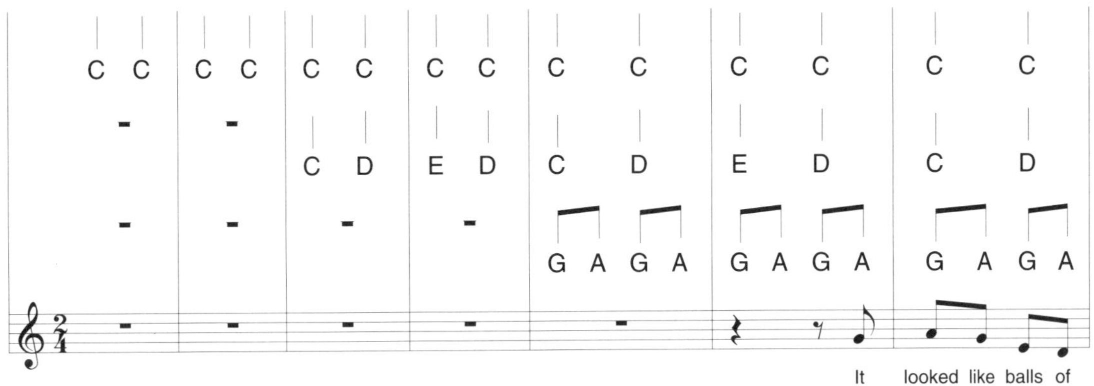

"It Was Snow" © 1978, 1980 by Sally Moomaw

4.13 Rain, Rain, Go Away

(Ensemble)

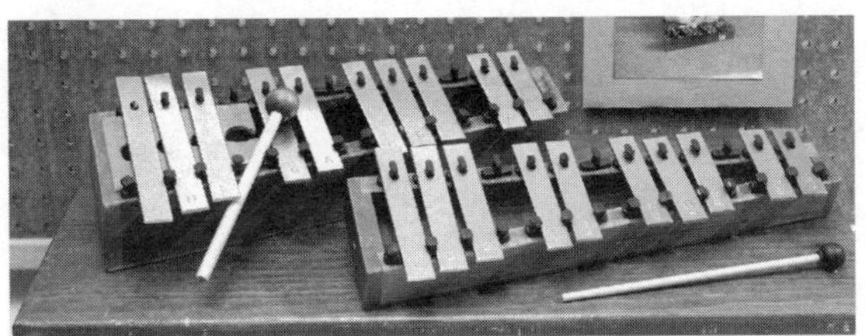

Child's Level

This activity is most appropriate for preschool or kindergarten children who have had many experiences with rhythm activities.

Description

This activity suggests a sequence of ostinato (repeated melodic pattern) accompaniments that children can play on Orff glockenspiels or xylophones.

For the initial ostinato, one child could play repeated eighth-note Gs. Then the group can join in singing the song as the ostinato continues.

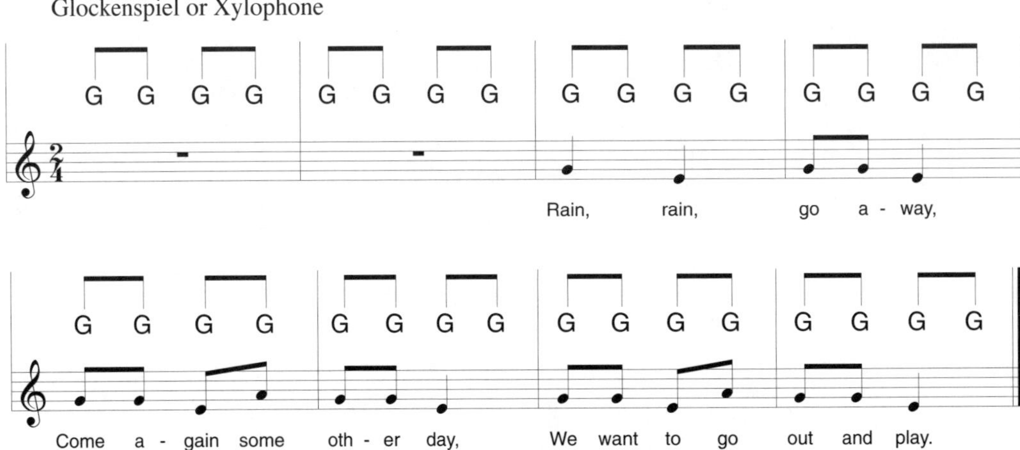

Later, introduce a second ostinato consisting of Cs on every other beat. The first child starts with the fast, repeated Gs, then the second child adds the slow, repeated Cs, and finally the rest of the children sing the song as the ostinati continue.

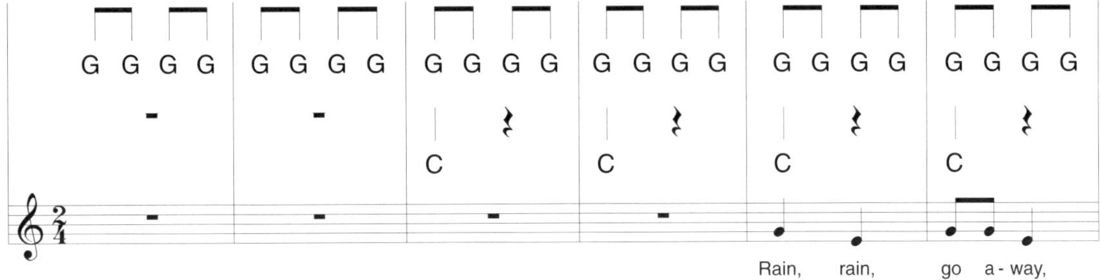

Finally, introduce a "walking" quarter-note ostinato, C D E G, as the third ostinato.

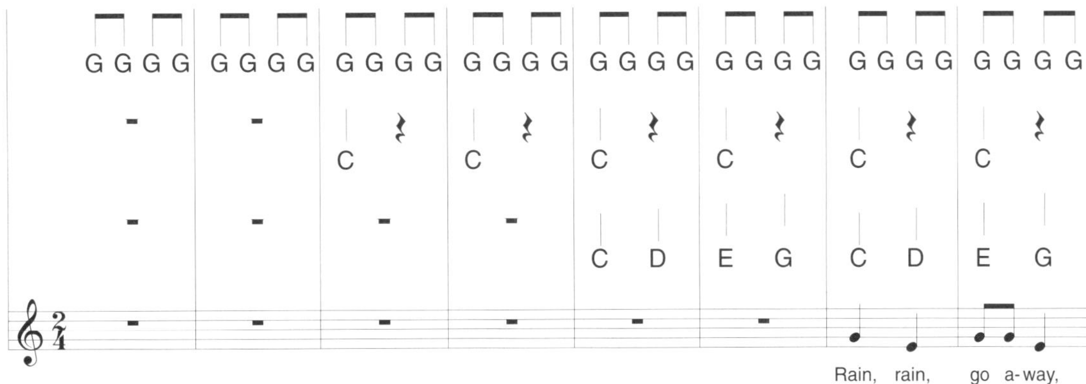

Extension

This simple tune lends itself to many different pentatonic ostinato combinations. Experiment with creating your own patterns. Encourage children to make up ostinati to try with the song.

4.14 Thunder
(Ensemble)

Child's Level

This activity is most appropriate for kindergarten children.

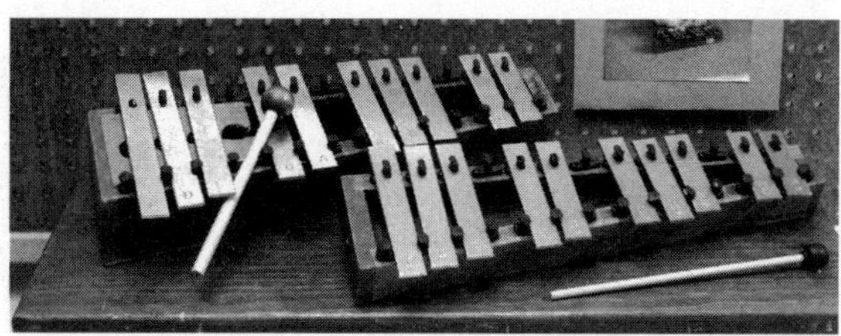

Description

This ensemble piece has three melodic ostinati plus a cymbal part. The melodic lines can be played on three Orff melody instruments (glockenspiels or xylophones, or any combination of the two). If three instruments are not available, two children can play their individual parts on the same xylophone. Several children can add cymbals as indicated. The children playing the cymbals have a more complex ostinato because, unlike a steady ostinato, they must wait for the appropriate time to play. If the children are already used to playing cymbals or drums at the end of each line (as in activity 2.10), then it will not be difficult to add the cymbal part to the ensemble.

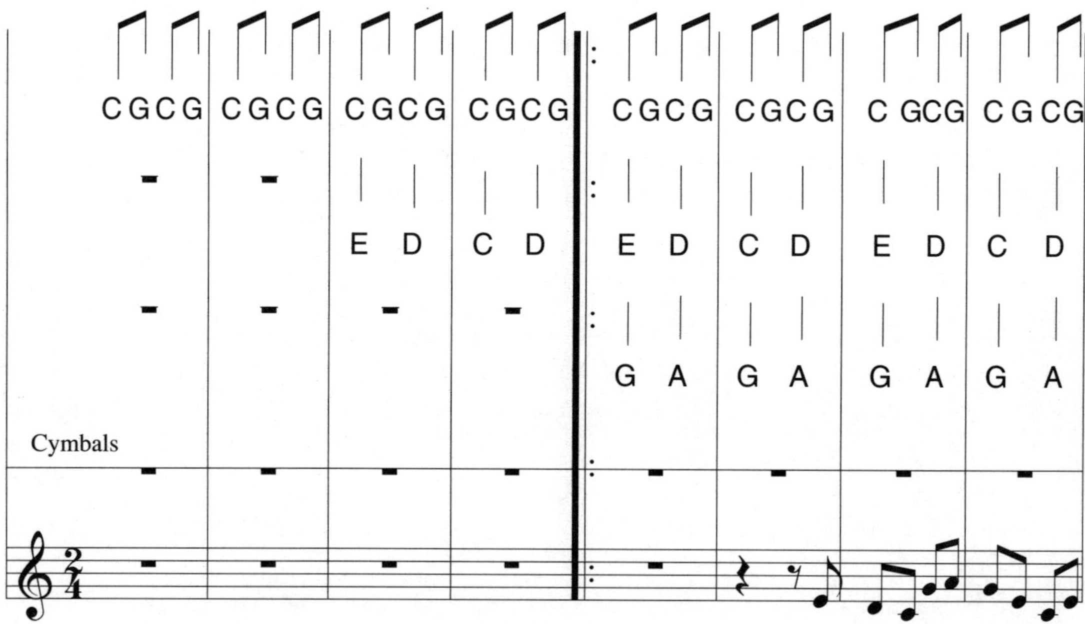

Modification

If this activity is too difficult, start with just one ostinato, as in activities 4.12 and 4.13. Add other patterns one at a time as the children are ready.

4.15 Music Listening Game

Description

Once children have had experiences with two or more instruments, they can begin distinguishing between the two auditorily. Start with two instruments with contrasting sounds, such as a wood block and a triangle. Hide the instruments behind a screen, such as a flannelboard or a pegboard divider, so the children cannot see the instruments. Play the instruments one at a time and let the children guess which one you are playing. Children become very excited when they realize they can identify the instrument by its sound and do not have to see it.

Child's Level

This activity is appropriate for either preschool or kindergarten children who are beginning to distinguish and play instruments.

Extensions

As the children have experiences with additional instruments, add them to the listening game. When children have had many opportunities to hear, see, and play the instruments, record the sounds of the instruments and put the tape in the music center. Children can identify the instruments used on the tape. Mount pictures of the instruments on note cards to help children remember the possibilities. Some children like to pick up the card for each instrument as they hear it on the tape.

Chapter 5

Music Centers

Kevin and Audrey were playing with hollow coconut shells in the music area. They had been there for some time and were beginning to get rough with the coconuts. The teacher came over, sat next to them on the floor, and commented that in the orchestra the coconut shells are used to make the sound of horses' hooves. Audrey and Kevin again played the shells but this time listened more carefully. They nodded and agreed that the shells did sound like horses' feet. At this point the teacher began a familiar chant, "Come Little Pony," and played the beats on her coconut shells. Audrey and Kevin immediately joined in, also playing the beats.

At the end of the chant the teacher asked why her coconut shells sounded softer than the children's coconut shells. Previously the teacher had displayed the coconuts with three types of beaters—rubber, wooden, and felt—so the children could experiment with how various materials affected the sound of the coconuts. However, so far these two children had not focused on the differences in the beaters. Audrey now listened attentively while watching the teacher's beater. "Oh!" she exclaimed. "Mine's loudest because it has wood, and then Kevin's because it's rubber, and then yours because yours is soft." Kevin agreed that this was true.

▲ ▲ ▲

Through experimenting with how sound is created, children form concepts about the nature of sound and music. They gain an awareness of how their actions alter sound. Teachers can encourage the construction of musical knowledge by providing many opportunities for children to explore sound.

Teachers' Questions

What is a music center?

A music center is an area of the classroom designed to encourage children to experiment with sound and music making. Although it is a permanent part of the classroom, the contents of the area are regularly changed to reflect the teacher's long-range goals, the interest of the children, and coordination with the overall curriculum.

Why is it important to include music centers in an early childhood classroom?

Music centers provide children with extensive time to explore the properties of sound and construct musical concepts. They also afford children the opportunity to create their own music. Children need blocks of time and repeated access to instruments in order to discover the properties of sound and explore their potential for creating music. This is not possible in a large group situation. The music area allows children to experiment with instruments frequently and over extended periods of time. Children may interact with the instruments individually or with other children.

What is included in a music center?

The music center includes a low bench or small table to hold several instruments. A divider or shelf sections off the area from the rest of the room and provides a space to hang related pictures and relevant print. A small wooden storage cabinet with a tape recorder, record player, or CD player is desirable. Since some instruments, such as chimes or triangles, need to be suspended, a small wooden frame to hold them is an ideal addition to the music center. The frame is easy to make. Screw four pieces of wood together (3½ inches wide by 20 inches long). Add two strips of wood to the bottom of the frame to keep it from tipping over. Attach hooks to the top of the frame for suspending the instruments. The frame is pictured in many of the activities in this chapter.

Since a primary goal of the music center is to encourage children to explore the sounds they can produce on musical instruments, the expectation is that the area will be somewhat noisy. It is therefore positioned away from quieter areas of the classroom, such as the reading and writing centers. While the area should be rather small and cozy, it should be large enough to accommodate two to three children comfortably. This allows for communal music-making and the exchange of ideas.

What kinds of activities are appropriate for a music center?

Teachers should include activities that encourage children to focus on specific attributes of instruments, such as size, the material of the instrument, and the way the sound is produced. A long-range plan allows for children to explore each of these aspects in a variety of ways over the course of the year. For example, children might begin by comparing the sound of two sizes of wood blocks. Next they might experiment with two sizes of triangles. As the year progresses, children could continue to explore the effect of size on sound by comparing various sizes of instruments or materials: drums, chimes, water glasses, xylophones, even flower pots or brake drums!

How long are the activities left out?

Children need repeated opportunities to return to instruments in order to construct musical knowledge. Therefore, each activity is usually left out for two to three weeks. Small changes or additions to the area may be made during this time, such as the addition of a third size of the same instrument or a different type of beater.

What musical concepts can young children construct?

Children can construct knowledge about pitch, dynamics, timbre, and tempo.

Pitch refers to how high or low a sound is. It is affected by the size of the vibrating body. Small instruments are higher in pitch than large instruments. The labels *high* and *low* refer to the number of vibrations per second; thus, a high sound indicates a high number of vibrations per second compared to a low sound. Children typically reverse these labels because they are perceptually bound. Since instruments with a low pitch are larger than instruments with a high pitch, they extend higher into the air and are often given a "high" label by children. Teachers can model the correct terms.

Dynamics indicates the volume of a sound (loud or soft). It is affected not only by the amount of force applied to an instrument, but also the material of the instrument and the tool used to play it. For example, a drum beater made of wood creates a louder sound than one made of soft felt. Children sometimes confuse the labels loud and high, so if they hear a sound that is both low and loud, they may call it high. Teachers can help by clarifying the terminology whenever appropriate.

Timbre is a musical term for tone quality. It is determined by the material used to make the instrument and the way the instrument is constructed. Children soon learn that instruments made of metal sound different from instruments made of wood.

Tempo indicates how fast or slow the music is performed. These concepts are explained in more detail on the specific activities in this chapter.

How can children create their own music?

Children often spontaneously make up songs, especially when they are in a music-rich classroom. Children can use melody instruments such as xylophones, glockenspiels, or electronic keyboards to create tunes. Orff xylophones and glockenspiels have removable bars. When teachers remove the bars labeled F and B, a pentatonic, or five-note scale, remains. When two children play instruments adjusted to this scale, anything they play sounds well together. Thus, children can create music with one another or share this experience with a teacher (see activity 5.14).

What is the teacher's role with regard to music centers?

The teacher plans what materials to put in the center based on her long-range goals, the interest of the children, or other aspects of the curriculum. The teacher can encourage children to focus on particular aspects of sound through her questions or comments. At the beginning of this chapter, the teacher directed Kevin's and Audrey's attention to the sound of the coconut shells through her comment about how they are used in the orchestra. Once interest had abated, she used a question to encourage them to compare the sounds produced by the various types of beaters. Suggestions of questions to extend children's thinking are listed with each activity.

How can teachers avoid management problems when incorporating music centers into the classroom?

Teachers should plan carefully for the location of the music area, start with durable instruments, and set consistent ground rules for the use of the instruments. The area should be located away from quiet areas where the music-making might disturb other children. It should also be separated from materials in the classroom that could damage the instruments, such as food, the water table, and excessive sunlight.

The music area is conceived as a place where children can explore materials and produce sound. Children's autonomy and self-expression are highly valued. For this reason, select durable materials, particularly during the beginning of the year. Because experiencing musical sounds and thereby enhancing the appreciation of music is also a valued goal for children, choose quality instruments rather than inexpensive toys. This does not necessarily entail a huge expense; quality wood blocks, triangles, drums, and finger cymbals are relatively inexpensive. Teach children ground rules from the first day of school for handling these real instruments. For example, the drums can be struck with several types of mallets but not thrown. This grounding allows children to independently explore the instruments for the rest of the year. Children learn quickly to appreciate the instruments if the teacher also values them.

Music Center Activities

5.1 Wood Blocks

Description

Wood blocks are hollow wooden cylinders or rectangular-shaped blocks. They produce a resonant sound when struck with a wooden beater. This music center has three wood blocks; two are the same size and one is smaller. This gives children the opportunity to explore the effect of size on the sound of an instrument. They can also use the wood blocks to play rhythms or accompany songs (see activity 4.1).

Musical Concept—Pitch

Children can construct basic concepts of pitch in music through exploring instruments that are identical except for size variations. In this music center, children can compare the sounds of instruments that are the same size with one that is smaller. The smaller wood block has a higher sound.

Child's Level

This center is appropriate for preschool or kindergarten children. It is an excellent first music center because the instruments are durable and require little supervision.

Questions To Extend Thinking

- ▲ Do any of these wood blocks sound the same?
- ▲ Do the big wood block and the small wood block sound the same or different?
- ▲ Why do you think this is called a wood block?

Modification

Add a third size of wood block once children have adequately explored two sizes.

Suggestions for Additional Activities

Use wood blocks for other activities, such as those listed in activity 4.1.

Have children make their own wood blocks. Help children saw a two-by-four to the desired length (5 to 6 inches is typical). This will be the bottom of the wood block. Also cut a piece of ¼-inch plywood the same length and width as the bottom piece. This will be the top of the wood block. Cut three small strips of plywood, each about ½-inch wide, so they are long enough to fit evenly along three edges of the bottom piece of wood. Glue the wood strips to the bottom piece of wood with wood glue, and then glue the top piece in place. Children can make beaters by gluing a macramé bead onto a 7-inch dowel that has the same diameter as the hole in the bead.

5.2 Mallet Medley

Description

Children quickly learn that each type of instrument has its own unique sound. Without experience, however, they may not realize that the type of mallet they use to play an instrument also affects the sound.

For this center, children have the opportunity to play a drum with five types of mallets, which are all easy to make.

Wooden—This is the most commonly used mallet. It is made from a macramé bead (¾ to 1 inch in diameter) and a wooden dowel. Choose a dowel that fits securely into the hole in the bead. Cut the dowel to a length of 7 inches. Use wood glue to secure the dowel to the inside of the bead. Wipe off any excess glue.

Hard Felt—This mallet produces a slightly softer sound than the wooden one. Make it exactly like the wooden mallet, but instead of wiping off the excess glue, place a small square of felt over the end of the bead and tie it in place around the bead. The glue will help hold the felt in place.

Soft Felt—This mallet makes a quieter sound than either the wood or hard felt mallets. Follow the instructions for the hard felt mallet, but add a layer of cotton balls or fiberfill in between the bead and the felt. This results in a softer surface and quieter tone.

Sponge—The sponge mallet is so soft that barely anything is heard, even if the child tries to play loudly. Cut a small piece of sponge, poke a hole in it, and glue it to a dowel.

Rubber—Rubber mallets make a resonant sound that is not as harsh as a wooden mallet. To make a rubber mallet, drill a hole in a hard rubber ball about 1 inch in diameter. Insert a 7-inch length of dowel into the hole and glue it in place.

Musical Concepts—Dynamics and Timbre

Children usually think that loudness or softness in music is governed solely by how much force one applies to an instrument. However, dynamics are also affected by the material used to play the instrument. Experimenting with mallets made of different materials allows children to construct this knowledge. The type of mallet also affects the tone color of the instrument.

Child's Level

This activity is appropriate for preschool or kindergarten children. Be sure that the tops cannot come off the mallets and pose a choking hazard for children who still put things in their mouths.

Questions To Extend Thinking

- ▲ Which mallet is it easiest to play soft music with?
- ▲ Which mallet makes the loudest sound?

Modification

Five mallets may be overwhelming for a first experience. You may choose to start with two or three and add others later.

Suggestions for Additional Activities

Children can experiment with how the type of mallet affects the sound of many different instruments. Wood blocks, chimes, and xylophones are examples of instruments that can be used with a variety of mallets.

5.3 Triangles

Description

For this center, three triangles are suspended from a wooden frame. (See page 124 for directions on making the frame.) Two of the triangles are the same size, and the third triangle is smaller.

Musical Concept–Pitch

This center allows children to again explore the effect of size on pitch, but this time with a metallic instrument. It is not only wooden instruments whose pitch is affected by size. The smaller triangle has a higher sound.

Child's Level

This center is appropriate for older preschool children or kindergartners. The triangle striker is not safe for younger children; however, they could use a large metal ring instead.

Questions To Extend Thinking

- ▲ What happens when you hold onto the triangle and don't let it dangle?
- ▲ Can you find two triangles that sound the same?
- ▲ Why do you think this triangle sounds different?

Modification

Add a third size of triangle once children have explored the differences between two sizes.

Suggestions for Additional Activities

Try the suggested activities listed for activity 4.2.

Plan additional activities where children can explore the relationship between size and pitch (see activities 5.9, 5.11, and 5.16).

5.4 Maracas

Description

Maracas, or rattles, come in many varieties and are used by cultures around the world. Clear plastic containers make resonant maracas and allow children to see what is inside the maraca producing the sound. For this center, partially fill 3½ -inch tall plastic jars with three different materials: beans, rice, and paper confetti.

Musical Concepts–Timbre and Dynamics

Experimenting with different fillers in the maracas helps children realize that the material inside a maraca affects the sound. It also determines how loudly the instrument can be played. The beans are much louder than the rice when the maracas are shaken with the same force. The paper confetti is very quiet no matter how hard the child shakes the maraca.

Child's Level

This activity is appropriate for all levels, from toddler through kindergarten. Be sure the lids are glued on securely, especially for the youngest children.

Questions To Extend Thinking

- ▲ Which maraca sounds the loudest? The softest?
- ▲ Which sound do you like the best?
- ▲ Can you think of other things that could go inside the maracas?

Modification

Children can suggest other fillers for the maracas. Add other maracas once children have experimented with the initial set.

Suggestions for Additional Activities

Make maracas with the children. Ask parents to contribute plastic bottles or jars and have children choose the fillers.

Keep the same filler, but change the container of the maraca. This also affects the sound. Children could compare metal, cardboard, and plastic maracas.

5.5 Shekere

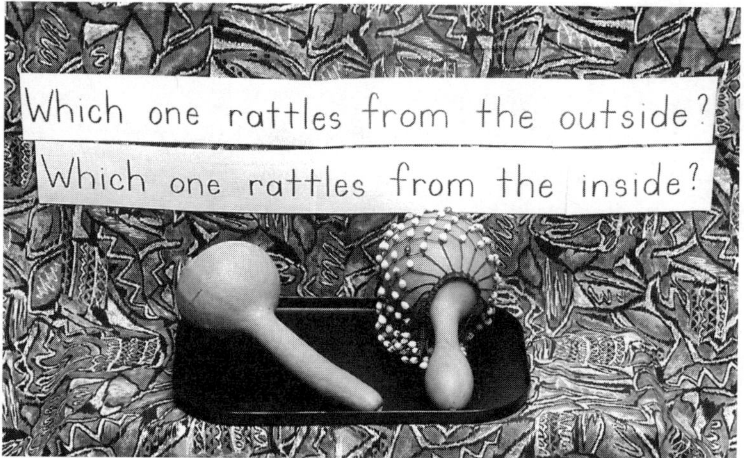

Description

The West African *shekere* is a maraca made from a dried long-necked squash and covered with a net of seeds. It originated with the Yoruba people of Nigeria. Children can compare the sound of the shekere with that of a similar dried gourd in this music center.

Musical Concept–Timbre

There are many types of maracas from around the world that children can explore. The shekere is especially intriguing because it rattles from the outside. It thus has its own special timbre.

Child's Level

The shekere is most appropriate for older preschool and kindergarten children who can better remember to shake it in the air and not "thunk" it against the ground.

Questions To Extend Thinking

- ▲ What do you think is making the sound of the shekere?
- ▲ What do you think is making the sound of the gourd?
- ▲ Do you think the shekere has anything inside it? Why or why not?

Modification
Add other types of dried gourds to the music center so children can compare the sounds.

Suggestions for Additional Activities
Let children experiment with making their own maracas (see activity 5.4).

Play recordings of African music during the day so children can hear the shekere and other African instruments.

5.6 Rainsticks

Description

Rainsticks come from the Diaguitas people of Chile. They are made from dried cactus. The tines of the cactus are pushed inside, and tiny pebbles are added. The pebbles make a lovely, tinkling sound as they drop through the cactus tines.

Musical Concepts—Timbre and Pitch

Rainsticks have a distinctive timbre that sounds like softly falling rain. The music center pictured in this activity has three sizes of rainsticks. Children can compare the relative pitch of the three instruments. The smallest rainstick sounds the highest.

Child's Level

This activity is most appropriate for older preschool or kindergarten children. Although the rainsticks are fairly durable, young preschoolers might bang them, which could cause them to break.

Questions To Extend Thinking

- ▲ What do you think is making the sound?
- ▲ Have we played any other instruments with something inside?
- ▲ Do the big rainstick and little rainstick sound the same?

Modification

Native American flute music makes a lovely addition to the rainsticks music center. Recordings such as *Dream Catcher,* by Kevin Locke, and *Changes,* by R. Carlos Nakai, are available.

Suggestions for Additional Activities

Use rainsticks to add tone color to rain songs.

5.7 Brake Drums

Description

Brake drums produce a ringing tone when struck with a mallet. Since there is some variation in the sizes of brake drums, a limited pitch variety can be obtained. This particular center uses two sizes of brake drums.

You can find discarded brake drums at a local junkyard. Thoroughly clean and then spray paint them. Be sure to paint them the same color so children do not mistakenly conclude that differences in the sounds are the result of the brake drums' color, rather than their size. Play the brake drums with either a wooden or hard rubber mallet.

Musical Concept—Pitch

Children usually notice that the two sizes of brake drums produce different pitches. The larger brake drum has a lower sound. Children also experience the clear, metallic tone of the brake drums.

Child's Level

Brake drums are appropriate for either preschool or kindergarten children. They are very heavy, so usually children are not inclined to try to lift them.

Questions To Extend Thinking

- ▲ Do the brake drums sound the same or different?
- ▲ What do you think the brake drums are made from?
- ▲ Have we played any other instruments made of metal?

Modification

After children have had the opportunity to explore the sound of the brake drums, introduce other types of mallets, such as hard and soft felt, so that children can explore the differences.

Suggestions for Additional Activities

Children can take turns using the brake drums to create tone color for songs sung at group time. Activity 2.3, which describes a fire truck, is an example.

5.8 Tongue Drum

Description

The African tongue drum is a hollow, rectangular wooden box. Slits cut through the top form "tongues" of varying lengths, which create different pitches when struck with a beater. The drum is very resonant.

You can order tongue drums from education or music catalogs, or make your own. To construct a tongue drum you'll need two pieces of wood for the top and bottom (6 by 18 inches each), two pieces for the sides (4 by 18 inches each), and two pieces for the ends (4 by 4½ inches each). In the piece of wood that will be the top of the drum, cut slits to form a lopsided, sideways H, as pictured. Then glue the drum together.

A hard rubber mallet works best for playing the drum because wooden mallets may put dents in the wood. Make a rubber mallet by drilling a hole in a 1-inch rubber ball and inserting and gluing a 12-inch piece of dowel to form the handle.

Musical Concepts—Timbre and Pitch

Children are eager to play the tongue drum because of its resonant sound. It is different from most drums because it is made entirely of wood. Children soon discover that the two "tongues" have different pitches. The long tongue sounds lower than the short tongue.

Child's Level

The tongue drum is appropriate for preschool or kindergarten children because it is very durable. Be sure children cannot pull off the end of the mallet and cause a choking hazard.

Questions To Extend Thinking

- ▲ What do you think the drum is made from?
- ▲ Have we played any other instruments made of wood?
- ▲ Do the two tongue parts have the same sound?

Modification

Construct a smaller version of the tongue drum to add to the music center. The smaller drum will also have distinct pitches, but higher ones than the larger drum if wood of the same thickness is used on both drums.

Suggestions for Additional Activities

Drums playing complex rhythms are a feature of music from many African cultures. Add recordings of African music to the music center to allow children to both listen and play along on the tongue drum.

5.9 Glissando Cans

Description

Glissando cans are metal containers partially filled with water, suspended from a wooden frame, and struck with a wooden beater. (The cans must have a top that closes securely; paint cans or varnish cans work well.) Children are intrigued with these instruments because of their unique sound.

For the music center, use two or three sizes of cans. Clean each can and add a small amount of water (about 1 inch for an 8-ounce can and 2 inches for a 1-quart can). Seal the tops securely. Spray paint the cans or cover them with contact paper to make them more attractive. Be sure to decorate the cans identically so that children do not get the mistaken idea that differences in sound are due to the color of the can. Suspend the cans from a wooden rack, as pictured, or from large hooks in a pegboard divider. Use large rubber bands or pipe cleaners to hold the cans.

Musical Concept—Pitch and Timbre

The glissando cans have a unique timbre. When struck with a beater, they give off a ringing tone that is altered by the sound of the water moving in the cans. The water creates a *glissando* effect, which means that the pitch slides up and down. The overall effect is lovely but somewhat spooky. The relative pitch of the cans is affected by their size. Thus, while all the cans slide up and down in pitch, the smallest can has an overall pitch that is higher than the larger can.

Child's Level

This activity is most appropriate for older preschool or kindergarten children.

Questions To Extend Thinking

- ▲ How does this instrument sound to you?
- ▲ What do you think is making the sound?
- ▲ Do the cans sound the same or different?

Modification

Once children have had ample time to explore the glissando cans, add a different type of beater, such as a soft felt one, so the children can compare the effect of the beater on the sound of the instrument.

Suggestions for Additional Activities

Explore the glissando effect with other instruments. Children can create glissandos on xylophones (activity 5.13), glockenspiels (activity 5.14), or chimes (activity 5.10) by moving the beater rapidly over all the bars. They can also move their fingers up and down a keyboard to create a glissando.

Children can also use slide whistles to produce glissandos. If the whistles are shared, sanitize them between uses.

5.10 Chimes

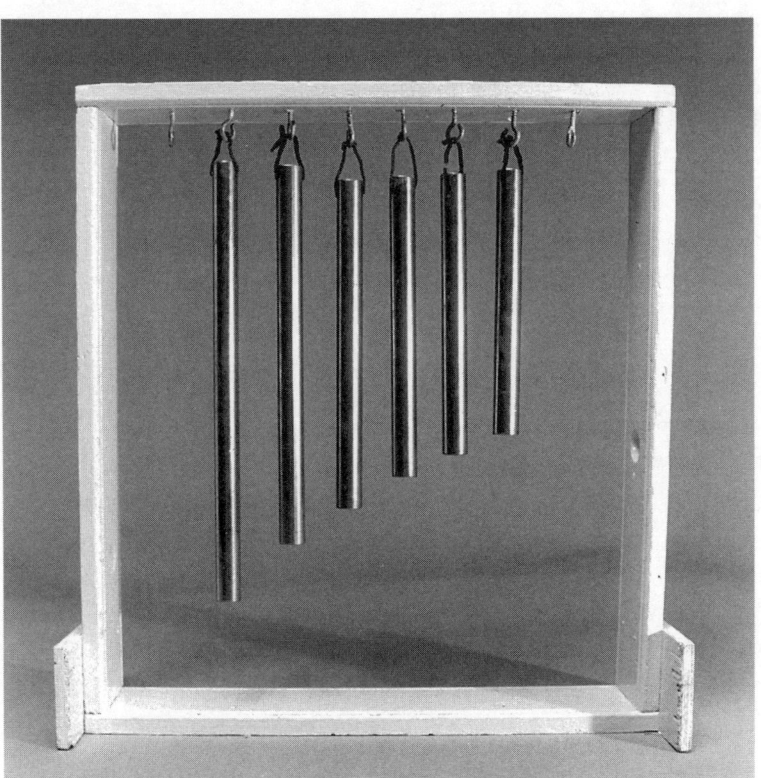

Description

Chimes are metal pipes of varying lengths suspended from a wooden frame so that they can resonate freely when struck with a mallet.

To make your own chimes, use either aluminum or copper 1-inch piping (both are found in hardware stores). Saw the pipe into assorted lengths and file the cut edges so they are not sharp. Drill a small hole through each pipe near the top so the bars can be suspended. Use pipe cleaners to hang the chimes from hooks on a wooden frame.

Musical Concept—Pitch

Although the chimes are not meant to be tuned to a specific scale, the varying lengths produce a range of pitches. Through repeated playing of the chimes, children learn that the pitch gets higher as the bars get shorter. Both aluminum and copper chimes make lovely sounds.

Child's Level

The chimes are appropriate for both preschool and kindergarten children.

Questions To Extend Thinking

- ▲ Which bar sounds the highest to you?
- ▲ Can we sing the sound that this bar makes?

Modification

After children have had time to experiment with the sound of the chimes, add beaters made of different materials, such as felt or rubber. Children can compare the results.

Suggestions for Additional Activities

Add recordings to the center so children can listen for chimes. The end of Tchaikovsky's *1812 Overture*, *Symphonie Fantastique* by Berlioz, and "Saturn" from Holst's *The Planets* are a few examples.

5.11 Flower Pots

Description

Clay flower pots produce a resonant sound when suspended from a frame and struck with a wooden mallet. Thread fishing line or twine through a macramé bead, position the bead on the inside of the hole at the bottom of the pot, and pull the cording through the hole. Invert the pots and hang them from hooks on a wooden frame.

Musical Concept–Timbre and Pitch

Clay pots provide a new sound medium for children to explore. They produce a ringing tone that differs from the sound of metal or wood. Flower pots of varying sizes give children another opportunity to construct the relationship between the size of an instrument and its relative pitch.

Child's Level

This activity is most appropriate for older preschool or kindergarten children.

Questions To Extend Thinking

- ▲ Which flower pot has the highest sound?
- ▲ Can you make a soft sound with the big flower pot?
- ▲ Can you make a loud sound with the little flower pot?

Modification

Extend this activity by supplying a variety of beaters (see activity 5.2). Children can construct how the material of the beater affects dynamics.

Suggestions for Additional Activities

Children might enjoy playing the flower pots for a chant about gardening. In the chant "Carrot, Carrot" (activity 3.12), they could play the flower pots on the words "It won't come up."

5.12 Multicultural Bells

Description

Many cultures have created lovely bells. This center allows children to explore various sizes of bells including jingle bells, bells from India, and bells from the Himalayas. You can purchase the bells (which are usually inexpensive) in import stores, gift shops, and craft supply stores.

Musical Concept—Timbre and Pitch

Each type of bell has its own unique sound. With repeated experience, children can learn to distinguish a jingle bell from a brass bell from India. Children can also discover that two bells of the same type that differ in size also vary in pitch, while two bells that are identical in both type and size sound the same.

Child's Level

The bells are most appropriate for older preschool or kindergarten children due to their small size.

Questions To Extend Thinking

- ▲ Can you find a bell that sounds exactly like this bell?
- ▲ Do you think the big jingle bell will sound the same as the little jingle bell or different?

Modification

Add a bell that is very different, such as a cowbell, once children are familiar with the original set of bells.

Suggestions for Additional Activities

Children can use bells to accompany lullaby songs (see activities 2.12 and 2.13).

Create listening games with the bells. After children have had experience with the bells in the music center, play the bells behind a flannelboard or other cover and let the children guess which bell you are playing.

5.13 Bamboo Xylophone

Description

The bamboo xylophone is inexpensive to make yet has a lovely tone. Many cultures employ forms of bamboo xylophones. For example, in Indonesia a similar instrument is called an *angklung*. Use a bamboo pole found at import stores or craft supply stores. Cut the bamboo at each joint to form the bars (which will vary in length). Suspend the bars above a board approximately 6 to 8 inches wide and 12 to 15 inches long, with about ½- to ¾-inch of space between the bars. Hammer 2-inch long nails into the wood between each bar at both the top and bottom of the wood frame. Suspend the bamboo bars by twisting rubber bands around each nail and bar. One rubber band will usually hold several bars. Be sure the bars do not hit the wood when struck with a beater or the sound will be distorted.

Musical Concepts–Timbre and Pitch

Bamboo has a resonant sound that is similar to wood but somewhat different. The bamboo xylophone gives children the opportunity to explore the timbre of bamboo. It is randomly pitched. In other words, the bars have specific pitches but do not conform to a traditional scale. Since each pole of bamboo will have joints of different lengths, no two instruments will sound exactly alike. The bars do not need to be placed in order according to length; however, children seem to have a strong urge to seriate them by size.

Child's Level

The bamboo xylophone is appropriate for older preschool or kindergarten children. Younger children may continually dismantle it.

Questions To Extend Thinking

- ▲ Can you think of any other instrument that sounds like this?
- ▲ Do the bars sound the same or different? Why?

Modification

Once the children have thoroughly explored the bamboo xylophone, introduce other types of beaters, such as felt or sponge, so that children can experiment with the effect of the material of the beater on the sound of the instrument.

Suggestions for Additional Activities

Bamboo is used to make flutes and panpipes in some cultures. You may wish to demonstrate Andean panpipes, which can be purchased at international stores, international festivals, through some catalogs, or at stores featuring Native American or South American materials.

Add recordings featuring bamboo xylophones, flutes, or panpipes to this music area.

5.14 Glockenspiels

Description

Glockenspiels are similar to xylophones but have metal bars instead of wooden ones. Quality glockenspiels have a beautiful tone. For this music center, the glockenspiels have been set to a five-tone, or pentatonic, scale. This is easily accomplished by simply removing the bars labeled F and B. Anything that children choose to play together on the two glockenspiels will sound harmonious due to the properties of the pentatonic scale.

Musical Concept—Pitch

Glockenspiels set to a pentatonic scale give children the chance to be composers—they can work together to create music. In the process, they also discover that the size of the bars alters the pitch. The longest bars are the lowest.

Child's Level

This center is appropriate for preschool or kindergarten children. It could continue to be used by children through elementary school.

Questions To Extend Thinking

- ▲ Which bar has the highest sound?
- ▲ Can you play the glockenspiel slowly?
- ▲ Can you think of any other instruments made of metal?
- ▲ Can you create a song with the glockenspiel?

Modification

After children have had the opportunity to create music with the glockenspiels, introduce different types of beaters, such as those in activity 5.2. Children can explore how the type of beater changes the sound of the glockenspiel.

Suggestions for Additional Activities

Use the glockenspiels to accompany songs (see activities 4.12, 4.13, and 4.14).

Children may wish to record some of their compositions.

5.15 Bottle Scale

Description

If you have a limited budget, you can make a melody instrument by filling identical glass bottles with varying depths of water and tuning them to correspond to the notes of a scale. The higher the level of water in the bottle, the lower the pitch. Experiment with how much water to add since the unique size and thickness of each bottle will affect the pitch.

Musical Concept–Pitch

The bottle scale gives children another way to explore the effect of size on pitch. They can use the bottles to create tunes.

Child's Level

This activity is most appropriate for older preschool and kindergarten children. Although the glass bottles seldom break, it is a possibility if they are mistreated.

Questions To Extend Thinking

- ▲ Do the bottles sound the same or different?
- ▲ All the bottles are glass—what do you think makes them sound different?

Modification

Add two glasses and a pitcher of water to the center. Children can experiment with changing the water depth in the glasses and observing the result. This could also be set up as a special activity where it could be more closely monitored.

Suggestions for Additional Activities

Children can play melodic patterns on water bottle scales to accompany songs (see activities 4.12, 4.13, and 4.14).

Children can make up songs on the bottle scale. They may wish to record them.

5.16 Lap Harp

Description

The lap harp is sometimes called a *zither*. It has a wooden frame and strings of graduated length. Children can use the lap harp to play tunes.

Musical Concepts—Timbre and Pitch

The lap harp gives children the chance to experiment with the sounds that strings create. String instruments have a timbre that is very different from other types of instruments. Children also discover that the length of the string affects the pitch. The longest string has the lowest sound. This is yet another medium for children to explore the relationship between size and relative pitch.

Child's Level

The lap harp is appropriate for either preschool or kindergarten children.

Questions To Extend Thinking

- ▲ What happens when you play different strings?
- ▲ Where do you have to play to get a high sound?
- ▲ How do you play loudly on the lap harp? Softly?

Modification

Add recordings of harp music to the music center once children have had time to explore the lap harp. Children may wish to compare the sounds of the lap harp with the harps on the recordings.

Suggestions for Additional Activities

Use the lap harp to play many of the songs in this book.

Children may wish to make up songs on the lap harp and record them.

CHAPTER 6

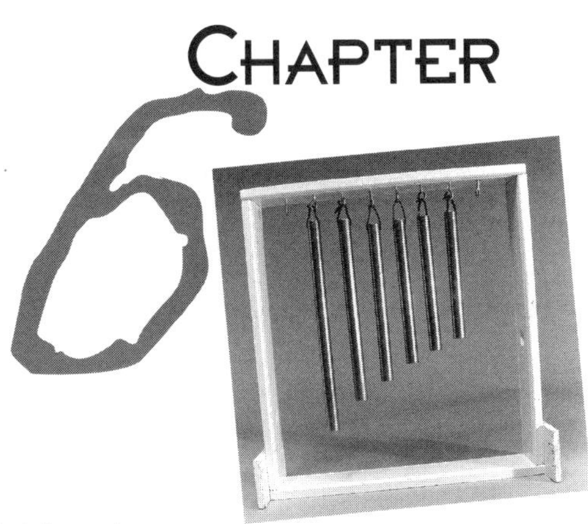

Movement

A group of toddlers was busily involved in classroom activities. A parent sat down with her autoharp in an open area of the room and began singing a song about rocking babies. Soon all of the toddlers clustered around her. They rocked back and forth and some began to join in the singing.

▲ ▲ ▲

Young children respond to music with their whole bodies. They eagerly dance, bend, and twist to the sounds they hear. Movement is an important way for children to explore and construct the rhythms, form, and emotion of music. They eagerly take advantage of the opportunity to add an aspect of themselves, their own physical interpretation, to the music. Since movement is central to the young child's exploration of music, it deserves careful planning and consideration by early childhood teachers.

Teachers' Questions

Why is it important to include movement activities in the curriculum?

Movement activities encourage children to experience music through their whole bodies, rather than just auditorily, and to respond creatively to music. This allows children additional avenues to explore the various moods and rhythms of music. Movement activities stimulate children to think imaginatively and provide for emotional release. They also help children develop better gross motor skills and body awareness since movement to music helps children orient themselves in relationship to space. Some activities emphasize particular parts of the body and specific movements.

What types of movement activities can teachers plan?

Teachers can include songs with specific directions and music that encourages dramatic interpretation. Songs with specific directions help children build language skills and allow teachers to focus on specific movements or parts of the body. This can be incorporated into specific goals for some inclusion children. Music that invites dramatic interpretation stimulates creativity and expressiveness in children. Both types of movement are included in the activities in this chapter.

What kinds of music encourage dramatization?

Children enjoy moving to music that dramatizes characters, suggests action, or creates a specific mood.

Many songs deal with people or animals familiar to young children. Songs about construction workers, gardeners, dogs, and birds are easy for many children to reenact because they have had many experiences with them. Children love the opportunity to use their imaginations and transform themselves into an animal they have seen or a person they admire. In addition to songs, teachers can use recordings of instrumental music to encourage dramatization of characters. Saint-Saën's *Carnival of the Animals* is one example.

Often music tells a story or suggests an action. In activity 2.3, "Fire Truck's on the Way," children can dramatize putting out a fire. They may wish to add new words to the last line, such as:

Out	jumps	______	to	put the	ladder	up	today.
Out	jumps	______	to	squirt the	water	on	today.
Out	jumps	______	to	roll the	hose	up	today.

These new words stimulate additional actions for children to use in portraying firefighters.

Some music creates a strong feeling of mood that children can portray through their movements. For example, Kevin Locke's Native American flute on his recording *Dream Catcher* evokes a peaceful feeling of rain, while a section of the overture to Rossini's opera *William Tell* depicts the tumult of a storm. Children can imitate rain falling in very different manners when comparing these two recordings.

What musical concepts can children construct through movement to music?

Children can gain a greater awareness and understanding of tempo, rhythm, and mood in music through movement activities.

Tempo refers to the speed of the music. Since children must match the speed of their movements to the tempo of the music, movement activities that focus on tempo help them listen more closely for this aspect of music. One of the best examples of alternating fast and slow tempos is Brahms's *Hungarian Dance* #5. Short, fast sections are followed by short, slow sections, with a marked contrast. Children can also explore *accelerando* (speeding up) and *decelerando* (slowing down), as in the song "Our Train" (activity 6.12).

Certain rhythms are associated with particular movements. For example, songs with a steady beat and a medium pace lend themselves well to walking or marching. Faster paced songs with a steady beat are good for running. Songs with a long-short, long-short rhythm suggest skipping or swaying back and forth.

Some music evokes a strong feeling of mood that children respond to in their movements. For example, the dances in Tchaikovsky's *Nutcracker Suite* differ markedly in character. Children quickly alter their movements as the music changes.

What is the teacher's role when leading movement activities?

The teacher's primary goal is to encourage the children to express themselves through movement. Teachers can also set guidelines to help children respect one another's space.

At first the teacher may need to take part in the movement activity to encourage children to move to music. As soon as possible, the teacher should withdraw and allow the children to express themselves; otherwise, they may just copy what the teacher is doing. The teacher may choose to take cues from the children and imitate their movements. Teachers can encourage creative dramatic movement by first discussing with the children how they think a particular character would move.

How often should teachers plan movement activities?

Some teachers like to plan daily movement activities; others incorporate movement once or twice a week. Movement activities encourage children to be actively involved with music. They also provide a change of pace during group times if children are becoming restless. Some teachers incorporate movement as a regular part of their day or as a portion of a longer group time.

How can teachers avoid management problems with movement activities?

Teachers need to set ground rules in advance so children know how much area they have to move around in. Some teachers provide a carpet square for each child to sit on during group times. For some movement activities, children may be asked to remain on their mats. At other times the children might move around the entire group time area or a large portion of the room. The teacher might remind them to keep their bodies from touching other children.

Teachers can pace movement activities so that when children become overly excited or active, another activity can be substituted to calm them down. For example, a teacher might plan to follow a movement activity with a quiet song.

What props can teachers use to encourage participation in music activities?

Teachers can employ a wide array of props to enhance movement activities. Scarves, ribbon streamers, finger puppets, nature items, and even Slinky spring toys are some of the possibilities. See the activities in this chapter for specific suggestions.

How can teachers use movement activities to help inclusion children?

Teachers can use movement activities to help children with orthopedic disabilities or motor delays isolate body movements and improve coordination within an inclusive and enjoyable context. For example, a child pretending to walk like a hippopotamus must alternate both sides of the body, but the exercise takes place among friends also interpreting the movements.

Teachers can also design movement activities to facilitate language development in children with language delays or among those just learning English. For example, if a teacher discovers that some children are having difficulty understanding prepositions, she might alter the words and movements in a familiar song such as "Put Your Finger on Your Nose" to emphasize prepositional phrases. For example:

Put your finger behind your back . . .
Put your finger over your head . . .
Put your finger in front of your knee . . .
Put your finger beside your head . . .

Although the song targets certain children, the entire class enjoys following the directions and performing the movements. See activity 6.11 for another version of this song.

Movement Activities

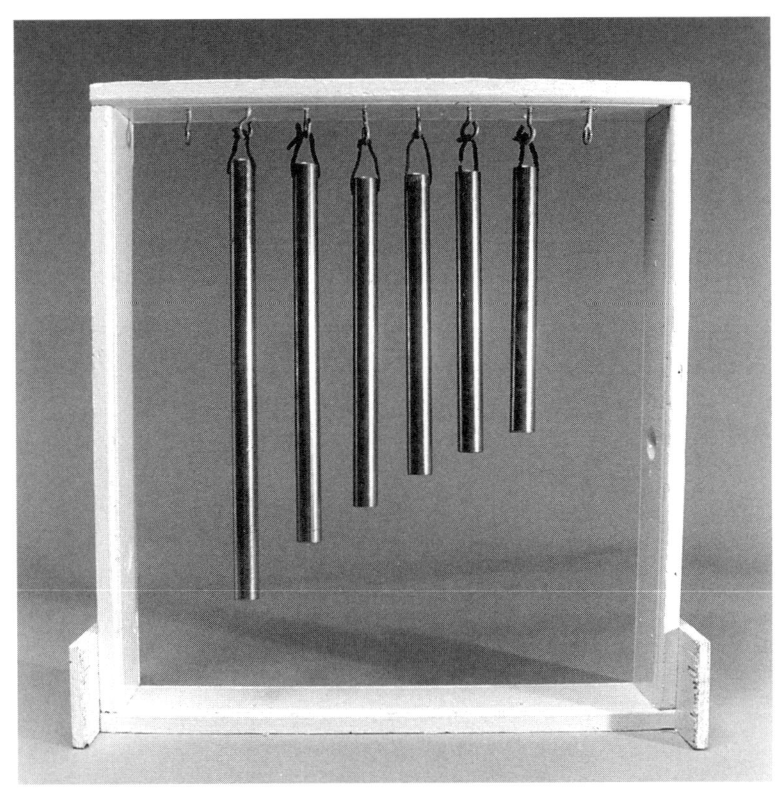

6.1 Stretching

Sally Moomaw
© 1996

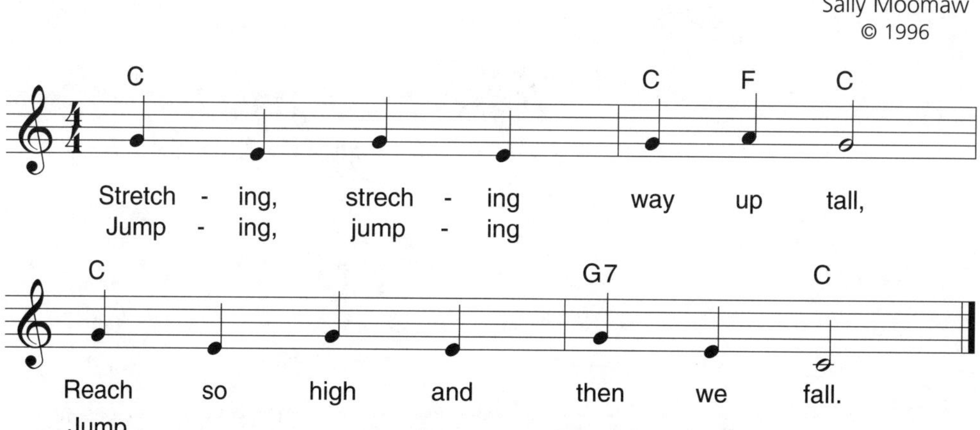

Description

Stretching and falling are two favorite activities of toddlers. This sentence song incorporates them both and has very simple directions for very young children.

Movement

This activity involves whole-body movement.

Child's Level

This song is most appropriate for toddlers.

Musical Extension

None recommended.

Integrated Curriculum Activities

Include books about toddlers and their activities in the book area. *All Fall Down*, *Clap Hands*, and *Tickle Tickle*, all by Helen Oxenbury, are examples.

6.2 Step, Step, Step

Sally Moomaw
© 1996

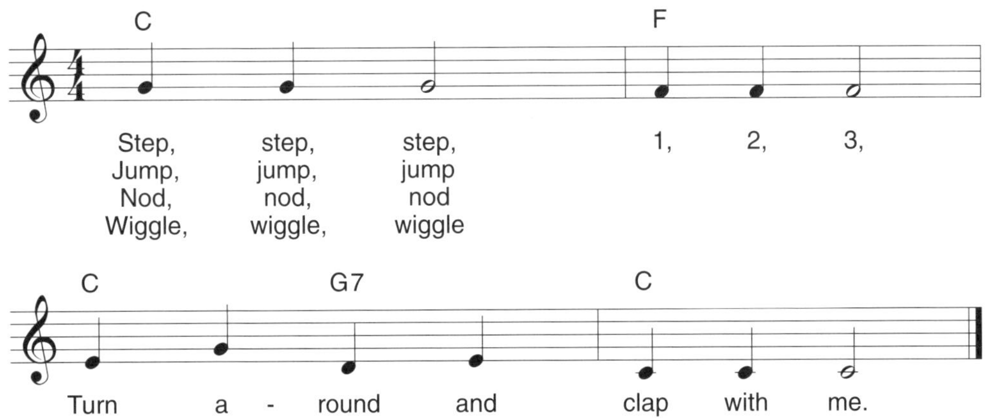

Description

Young children enjoy following the directions in this song as they move to the music. Children can suggest additional movements to add to the song.

Movement

This activity incorporates large body movements. You can include specific movements to meet the needs of individual children.

Child's Level

This activity is most appropriate for toddlers or young preschoolers due to its short length.

Musical Extension

Children can play the beats of this song on wood blocks. Change the word *step* to *tap*.

Integrated Curriculum Activities

Informally include the song when children are involved in gross-motor activities, such as climbing steps or jumping on trampolines.

6.3 Leaves Falling

Sally Moomaw

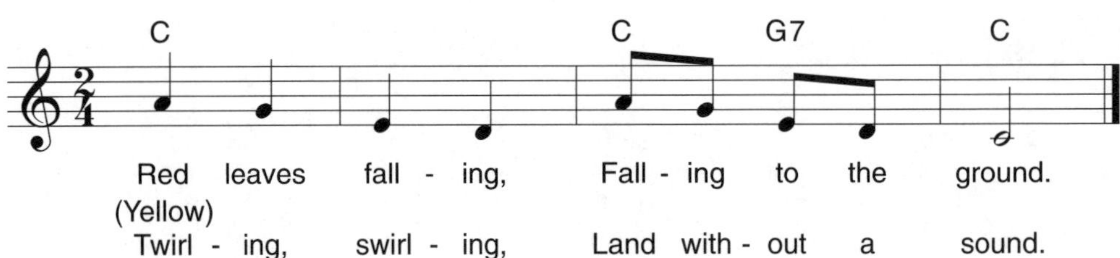

Props

▲ real leaves, or leaf shapes cut from colored paper

Description

Children can drop their leaves, watch them fall, and then fall like the leaf as you sing the song.

Movement

Young children use their whole bodies to imitate the leaves. At another time, you could have the children remain seated and act out the leaves falling with their hands and arms.

Child's Level

This song is most appropriate for toddlers or young preschool children due to its short length.

Musical Extension

Children can create the swishing sound of leaves blowing by using maracas made from clear plastic bottles and filled with rice.

Integrated Curriculum Activities

Take a nature walk and collect leaves.
Use leaves for collage activities.
Put tongs, buckets, leaves, and nature items in the sensory table.

6.4 Turtle

Sally Moomaw
© 1996

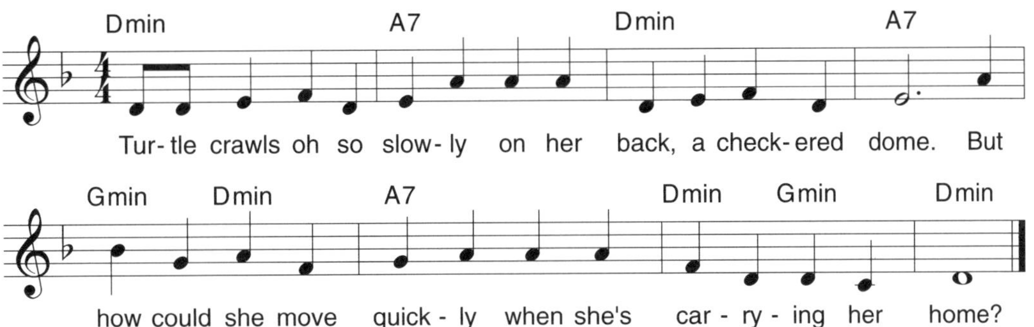

Description

When asked to imitate the turtle in this song, children often spontaneously put their group-time mats on their backs and begin to crawl around.

Movement

Encourage the children to interpret the song freely using their whole bodies. This is a good activity to focus children's attention on tempo in music, since it moves so slowly.

Child's Level

This song is appropriate for either preschool or kindergarten children.

Musical Extension

Children can use scraping instruments, such as shells with ridges or wood blocks with grooves, to accompany this song (see activity 4.7).

Integrated Curriculum Activities

Take a field trip to a nature area, pet store, or zoo to observe turtles.

Add word cards for animals with shells (such as turtle, snail, and crab) to the writing center.

6.5 Caterpillar

Sing to the tune of "Twinkle, Twinkle, Little Star" (see page 14 for the music):

Caterpillar in the woods,
Eating leaves that taste so good.
If you watch him by and by,
He'll become a butterfly.
Caterpillar in the woods,
Eating leaves that taste so good.

additional verses by Sally Moomaw

2. Caterpillar inches up a tree,
   He won't stop to wait for me.
   If you watch him by and by,
   He'll become a butterfly.
   Caterpillar inches up a tree,
   He won't stop to wait for me.

3. Caterpillar crawls across a twig,
   He's eating a lot, he's getting big.
   If you watch him by and by,
   He'll become a butterfly.
   Caterpillar crawls across a twig,
   He's eating a lot, he's getting big.

4. Caterpillar on the ground,
   Made his body nice and round.
   If you watch him by and by,
   He'll become a butterfly.
   Caterpillar on the ground,
   Made his body nice and round.

5. Caterpillar spun a cocoon,
   It's cold outside, so he's none too soon.
   If you watch him by and by,
   He'll become a butterfly.
   Caterpillar spun a cocoon,
   It's cold outside, so he's none too soon.

Props

- ▲ Slinky spring toys

Description

Children can use the spring toys to dramatize the caterpillar as it inches up a tree, makes a ball on the ground, and performs any other movements they may choose to add.

Movement

This activity emphasizes small body movements as children use the spring toys to reenact the song. Use the same song for large body movements by having the children pretend to be the caterpillar and move accordingly.

Child's Level

This song is appropriate for either preschool or kindergarten children.

Thanks to Dawn Denno for this idea.

Musical Extension

Slinky spring toys make excellent rhythmic devices. Children can click them together to play the beats in the song.

Integrated Curriculum Activities

Read books about caterpillars, such as *The Very Hungry Caterpillar,* by Eric Carle.

If possible, bring real caterpillars into the classroom.

6.6 Soft White Snowflakes

Sally Moomaw

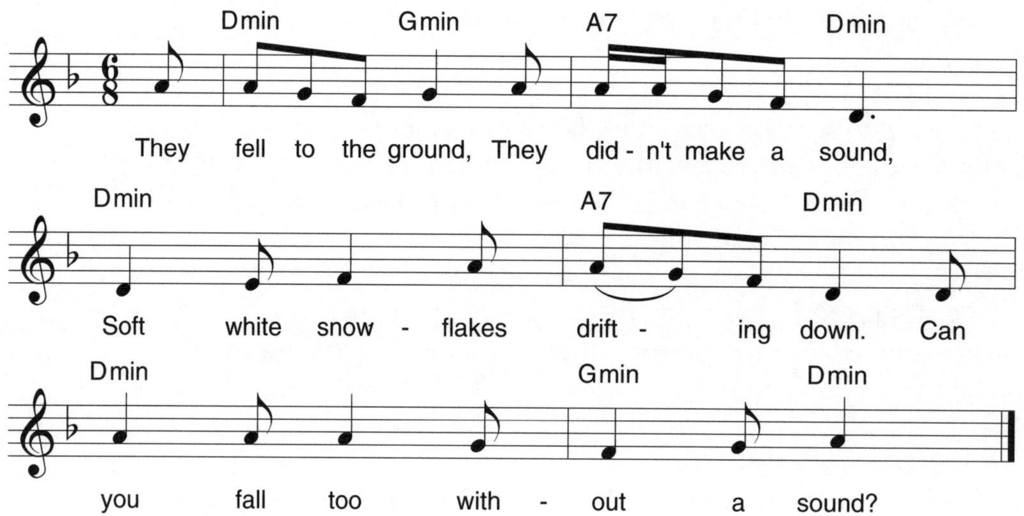

Additional verses
2. They swirled in the air…
3. They danced up and down…
4. They lay on the ground…
5. They blew left and right…
6. They melted in the sun…

Props

▲ white paper doilies or snowflake cut-outs

Description

Children can use their whole bodies to reenact the motions of the snowflakes. They can either drop the paper snowflakes and watch them fall before imitating the movement, or they may hold them in their hands as they dance.

Movement

This song encourages children to move their whole bodies creatively as they imitate the snowflakes. You can also use it as a finger play with small-motor movements.

Child's Level

This song is appropriate for either preschool or kindergarten after the children have experienced snow.

Musical Extension

Children can play softly on finger cymbals, triangles, or bells to accompany this song after they have first clapped the beats.

Integrated Curriculum Activities

Put snow in the sensory table with buckets and scoops.
Use cookie cutters to make playdough snowmen.
Sing other snow songs (see activities 2.6 and 4.5).
Read books about snow, such as *The Mitten,* by Jan Brett, *Andy, An Alaskan Tale,* by Susan Welsh-Smith, and *In the Snow,* by Huy Voun Lee.
Add wooden snowmen to the block area.
Create snow math games (see *More Than Counting,* by Sally Moomaw and Brenda Hieronymus, activities 4,16, 5.10, and 5.21).

6.7 The Hippopotamus

Patricia Bevan
Used by permission

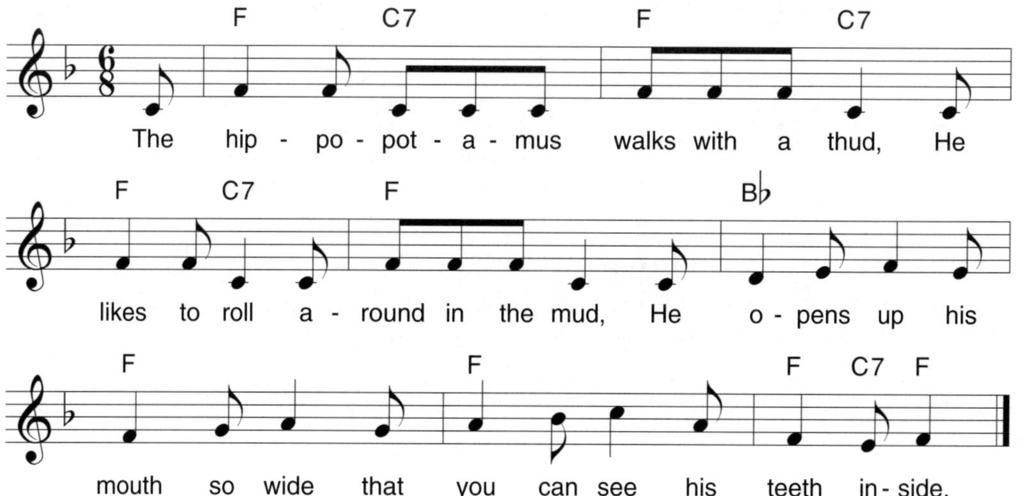

Description

The descriptive words of this song invite dramatization. Because ample space is needed for the hippos to roll around, you may choose to have several children at a time act out the hippopotamus rather than the entire class.

Movement

The dramatic movements inspired by this song encourage large body movements and use of both sides of the body. This can be especially helpful for children who have a weakness on one side.

Child's Level

This song is most appropriate for preschool children, although kindergarten children also enjoy the descriptive words.

Musical Extension

Children can create the thumping sound of a hippopotamus' walk by playing the beats on drums.

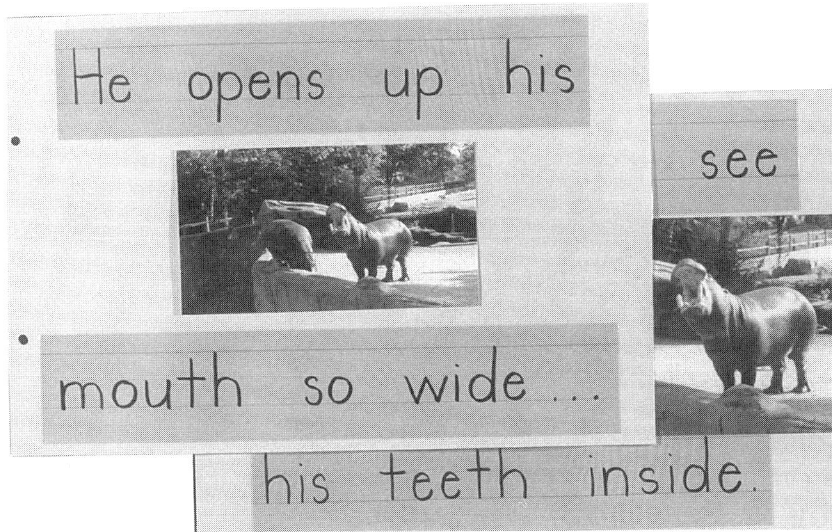

Whole-Language Extension—Big Book

Materials

- ▲ 6 pieces of construction paper, 12 by 18 inches each
- ▲ sentence strips
- ▲ illustrations of hippos

Description

This song is very popular with preschoolers and therefore makes a good big book. Print the words to the song on sentence strips. Allow one line of the song for each page of the book, for a total of four pages, plus front and back pages. Illustrate with pictures of hippos.

Integrated Curriculum Activities

Read zoo books, such as *Dear Zoo,* by Rod Campbell, *A Children's Zoo,* by Tana Hoban, and *What Happens at the Zoo,* by Judith E. Rinard.

Put zoo animals in the block area.

Include zoo animal word cards in the writing area along with blank books shaped like animals.

Play the rhythms of zoo animal names (see activity 4.1).

Use zoo animal cookie cutters with playdough.

6.8 5 Brown Acorns

Sally Moomaw
© 1996

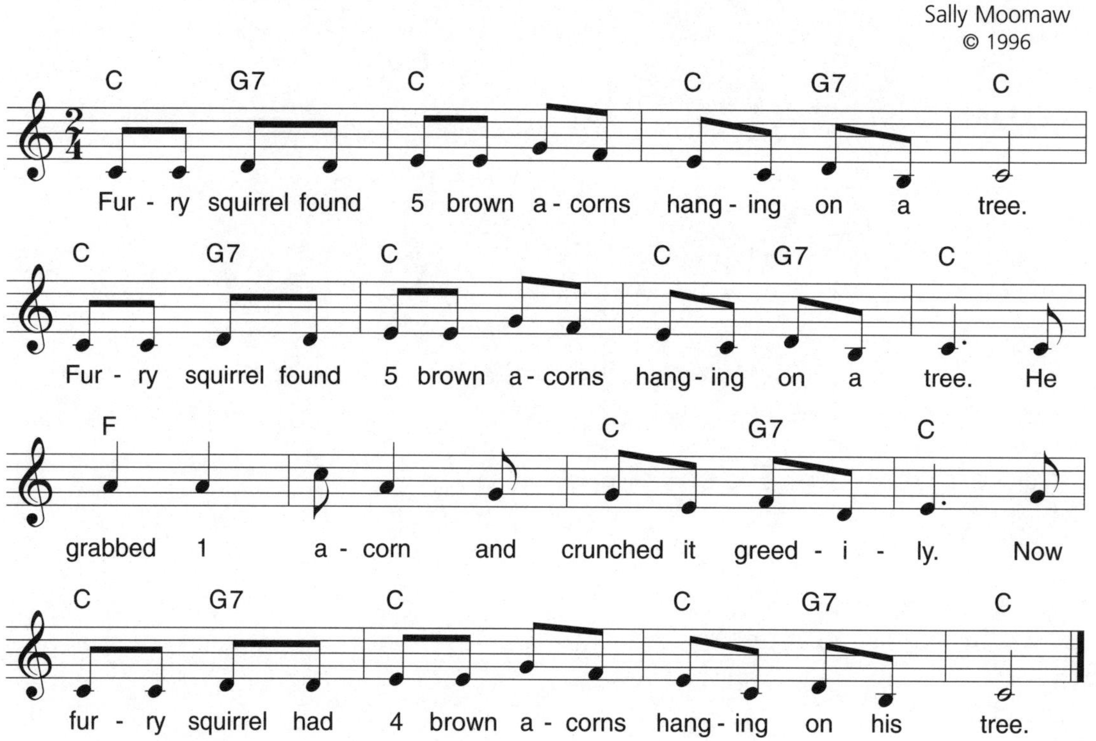

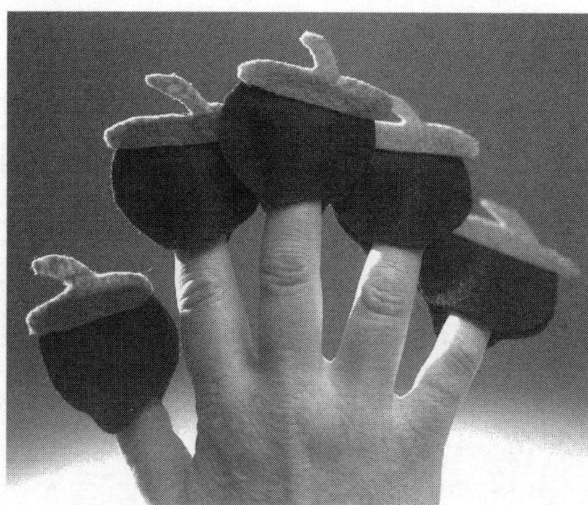

Props

- ▲ 5 acorn finger puppets per child, cut from brown and tan felt and sewn along the edges

Description

Children can perform this song as a finger play or use the finger puppets to help them dramatize the action. This song makes an excellent math activity.

Movement

This activity incorporates small-motor movements as children assemble the acorns on their fingers and pick them one at a time.

Child's Level

This activity is most appropriate for older preschool or kindergarten children. Younger children may find it frustrating trying to get the finger puppets onto their fingers.

Musical Extension

Children can play wood blocks on the words "crunched it greedily" to imitate the sound of acorns cracking.

Integrated Curriculum Activities

Make a math grid using squirrel stickers for the grid boards and acorns for the counters (see *More Than Counting,* by Sally Moomaw and Brenda Hieronymus, activity 4.5).

Add tongs and assorted nuts to the sensory table. Children can sort them into bowls.

Read books about squirrels, such as *Nuts to You!,* by Lois Ehlert.

Sing other fall songs (activities 2.5 and 6.3).

Crack open nuts with a block of wood as a science activity or for nut tasting.

6.9 5 Little Ducks

Traditional

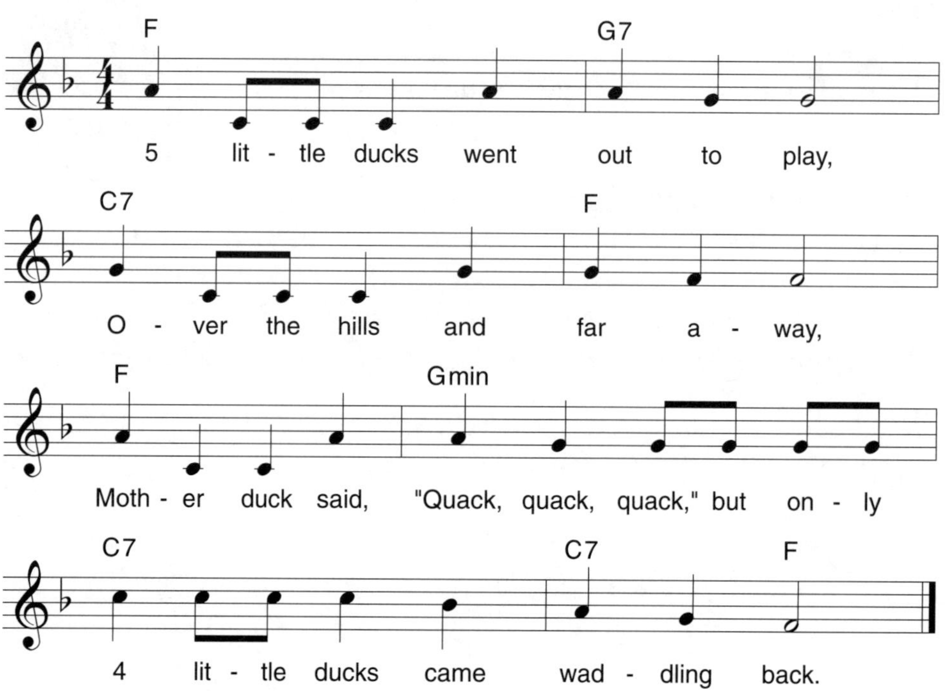

4 little ducks went out to play,
Over the hills and far away,
Mother duck said, "Quack, quack, quack,"
But only 3 little ducks came waddling back.

3 little ducks…
But only 2 little ducks…

2 little ducks…
But only 1 little duck…

1 little duck…
But no little ducks…

No little ducks went out to play,
Over the hills and far away,
Mother duck said, "QUACK, QUACK, QUACK,"
And 5 little ducks came waddling back.

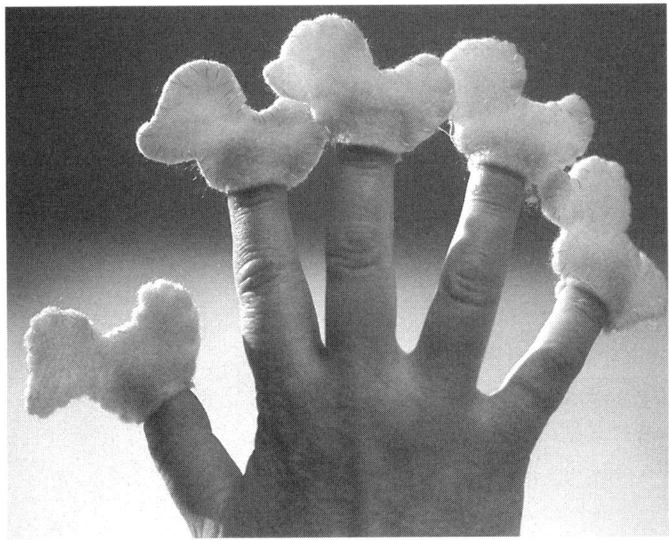

Props

- ▲ finger puppet ducks cut from yellow felt and sewn or glued around the edges

Description

Children can use the finger puppets to dramatize the words to this familiar song. It also makes an excellent math activity.

Movement

"5 Little Ducks" is traditionally sung as a finger play and therefore involves small body movements. You can also design a large-motor activity by designating five children at a time to dramatize the ducks in the song.

Child's Level

This activity is most appropriate for older preschool or kindergarten children. The vocal range is a bit wide for young preschoolers.

Musical Extension

Children can add tone color to the song by playing kazoos on the "quack, quack, quack" words in the song.

Integrated Curriculum Activities

Add rubber ducks to the sensory table.

Include a book version of the song in the book area, such as "Five Little Ducks" from *Raffi Songs to Read*.

Use duck cookie cutters and yellow paint as a printing activity.

6.10 Little Mouse

Sally Moomaw
© 1996

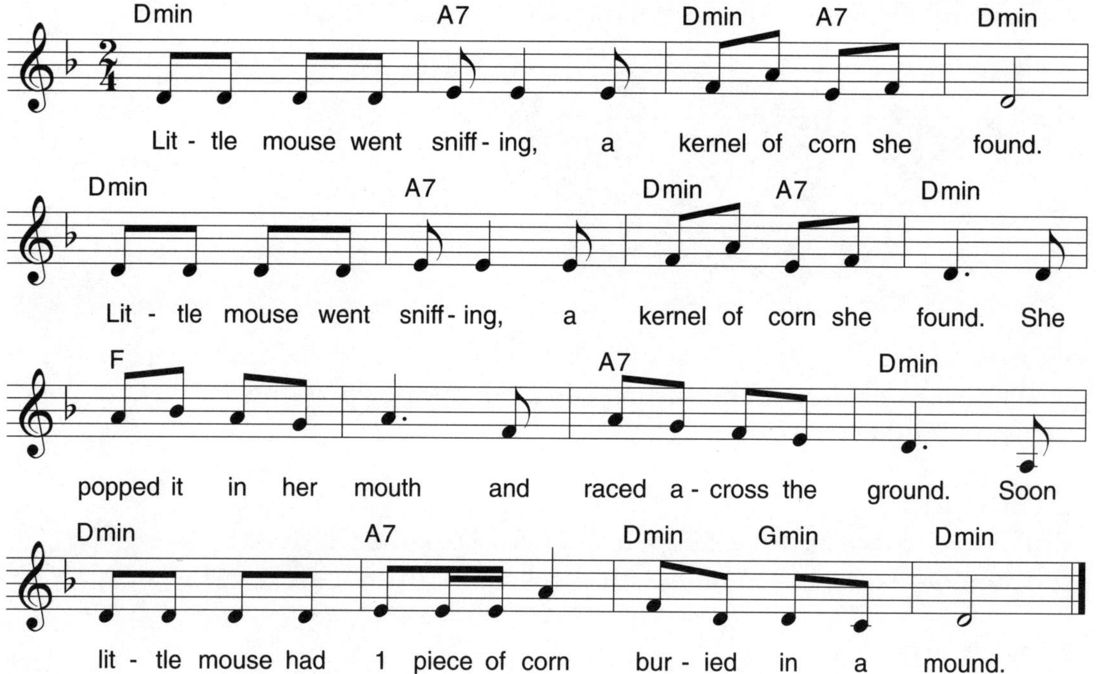

Props

- ▲ kernels of corn
- ▲ tiny mouse ears on elastic cord
- ▲ brown felt squares

Description

Children can dramatize this song by pressing their forefinger and thumb together to make the mouse. The props encourage children to reenact the words to the song. The mouse ears are circles cut from gray felt and sewn to a ring of elastic that fits over the child's finger. Place a felt square in front of each child to represent the mound of dirt. Children can bring one kernel of corn to the mound each time they sing a verse of the song. It is an excellent math activity.

Movement

This song encourages small body movements as children move their mice and pick up kernels of corn. Children can remain seated for this activity. You may also choose to use this song for large body movements by having children pretend to be mice.

Child's Level

This song is most appropriate for older preschool or kindergarten children because of the tiny pieces of corn.

Musical Extension

Children can accompany this song with corn maracas (see activity 4.3).

Integrated Curriculum Activities

Read books about mice, such as *Mouse Paint,* by Ellen Stoll Walsh, and *Two Tiny Mice,* by Alan Baker.
Put corn in the sensory table with large-hole funnels and buckets.
Add dried corn to the science area. Children can use tweezers to pluck the kernels from the cob.
Include corn on the art shelf for collages.
Use dried corn on the cob as a painting tool.

6.11 There's a Rabbit

(Inclusion Activity)

words by Sally Moomaw
Traditional tune, "Put Your Finger on Your Nose"
Lyrics © 1996

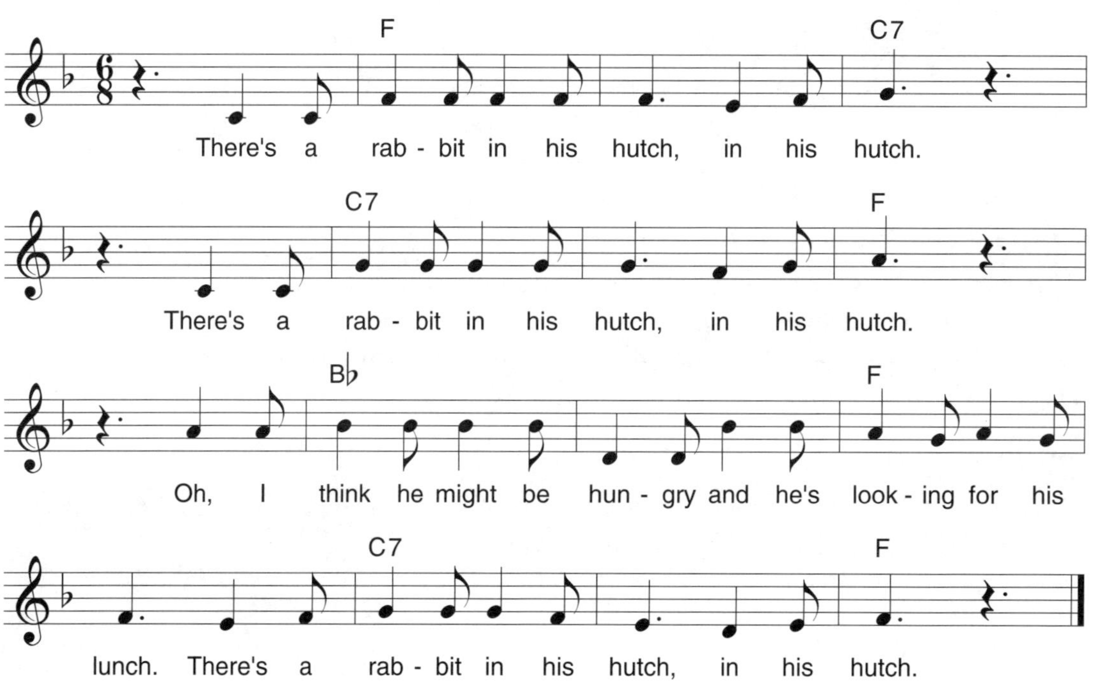

Additional verses
2. Now the rabbit's behind the hutch, behind the hutch…
3. Now the rabbit's in front of the hutch, in front of the hutch…
4. Now the rabbit's next to the hutch, next to the hutch…

Props

- ▲ a small rabbit for each child (found at craft or novelty stores or in sets as math counters)
- ▲ a plastic vegetable basket from the grocery store for each child

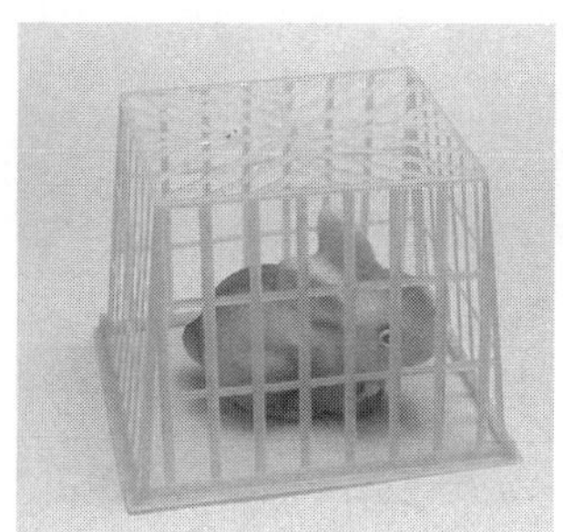

Description

This song helps children with English as a second language or with language delays focus on the meaning of prepositions. Although certain children may be targeted with this activity, it is popular with all. The song originated with a class that had a pet rabbit. Alter the words to describe a pet from your class or an animal you are studying.

Movement

This activity is designed to emphasize small body movements so children can visualize the placement of the rabbit. Children can also take turns being the rabbit, perhaps in the gross-motor area with a box or block structure for the hutch.

Child's Level

This song is appropriate for both preschool and kindergarten children, although the large skips in the melody make it more difficult for young preschoolers to sing.

Musical Extension

None recommended.

Integrated Curriculum Activities

Use rabbit cookie cutters with playdough.

Make a rabbit grid math game using rabbit stickers for the grid and carrot erasers for the counters (see *More Than Counting,* by Sally Moomaw and Brenda Hieronymus, activity 4.3).

6.12 Our Train

Sally Moomaw

Description

This activity involves the whole group in a unified endeavor. Children join hands behind you to form a train. As the group moves around the room, it starts slowly, gradually speeds up, and then slows down again as the train nears the station and the song ends.

Movement

This activity involves gross-motor movements and coordination of individual body actions to fit in with a group. This is tricky for some children. The activity also requires children to listen for the changes in tempo and adjust their movements accordingly.

Child's Level

This song is appropriate for either preschool or kindergarten children.

Musical Extension

This activity emphasizes the musical concepts of *accelerando* (gradually speeding up) and *decelerando* (gradually slowing down). Children can re-create the sound of the train with scraping instruments, such as wood blocks or rhythm sticks with grooves. They can scrape the instruments on the beats and focus on speeding up and slowing down with the music.

Integrated Curriculum Activities

Add trains to the block area.

Paint pictures by dipping small trains in paint and rolling them over the paper.

Read books about trains, such as *Freight Train,* by Donald Crews, *The Train Ride,* by June Crebbin, and *Trains,* by Byron Barton.

Listen to recordings that illustrate accelerando, such as Grieg's "In the Hall of the Mountain King" from *Peer Gynt*.

6.13 Dance Myself Dizzy

Peter Moomaw

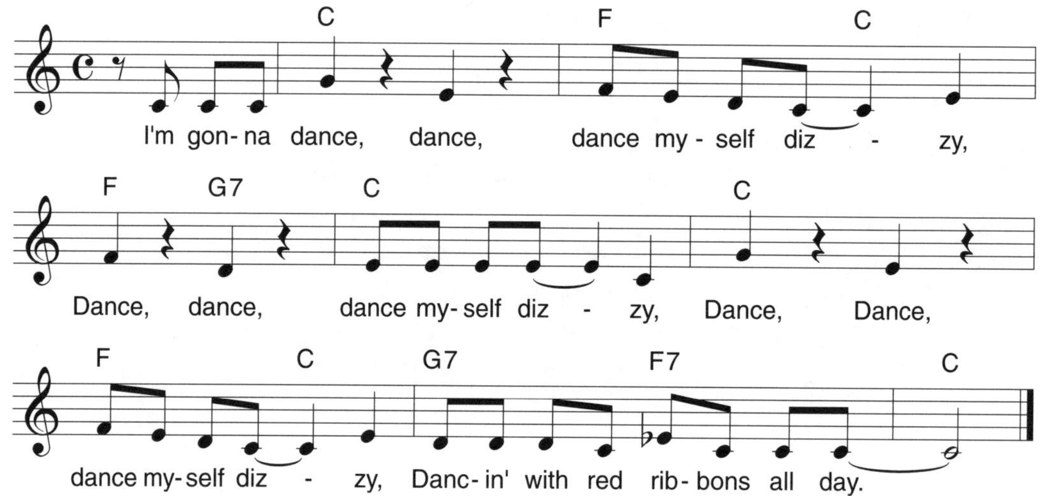

Props

- ▲ plastic bracelets found in party favor departments or craft stores
- ▲ ribbons cut in 2-foot lengths and sewn to the bracelets

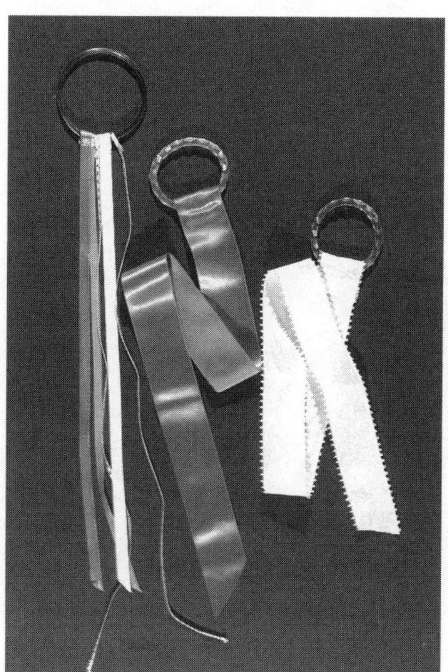

Description

Ribbon streamers attached to plastic bracelets make excellent props for creative movement activities.

Movement

Children are encouraged to move creatively as they watch their ribbon streamers move with them.

Child's Level

This activity is popular with both preschool and kindergarten children.

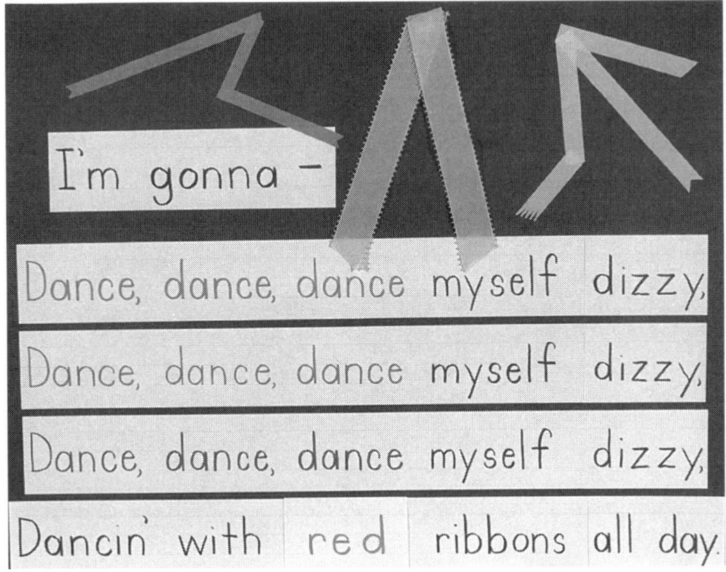

Whole-Language Extension–Interactive Chart

Materials

- ▲ black poster board, 22 by 28 inches
- ▲ sentence strips
- ▲ brightly colored ribbon

Description

Print the words of the song on sentence strips, as illustrated. The color words are the interactive words. Illustrate the chart with pieces of brightly colored ribbon and a picture of a dancer, if desired.

Integrated Curriculum Activities

Include dance books, such as *Dancing with the Indians,* by Angela Shelf Medearis, and *Color Dance,* by Ann Jonas, in the reading area.

Make ribbon collages in the art area, or use ribbons to weave into the frames of plastic vegetable baskets.

Set up a dance studio in the dramatic play area (see activity 6.15).

6.14 Rainbows of Color

Sally Moomaw

Props

- ▲ colored chiffon scarves

Description

Children can wave scarves through the air as they sway to the sounds of this song. As the scarves cross, children can see new colors emerge. This activity coordinates well with the book *Color Dance,* by Ann Jonas, where children also dance with scarves.

Movement

This song suggests whole-body movements of swaying and turning, back and forth, to the rhythm. Arm movements are encouraged as children move the scarves. You can emphasize low and high, forward and back, and left and right.

Child's Level

This song is appropriate for either preschool or kindergarten children.

Musical Extension

Some children can play the beats on finger cymbals or triangles while others dance with the scarves.

Whole-Language Extension—Interactive Chart

Materials

- ▲ white poster board, 28 by 22 inches
- ▲ colored markers
- ▲ rainbow illustration
- ▲ scarf shapes cut from cellophane
- ▲ scarf shapes cut from colored construction paper

Description

Print the words to the song directly onto the poster board, as pictured. Use a different color for each line, if desired. Leave a space for each of the three color words in line three. Children can add the scarf cut-outs with the appropriate color printed on them to the chart. Laminate the chart and scarf pieces. Attach the interactive scarf word cards to the chart with Velcro, magnetic tape, or a paper fastener.

Integrated Curriculum Activities

Read other books about mixing colors, such as *Mouse Paint,* by Ellen Stoll Walsh, and *Little Blue and Little Yellow,* by Leo Lionni.

Mix colors at the easel. Use tiny spray bottles filled with colored water.

Add a dance area to the dramatic play area (see activity 6.15).

6.15 Dance Area

Description

Children love the experience of having a dance area in the classroom. Since dancing is an important part of many cultures, a dance unit is an excellent multicultural activity. You can easily convert the dramatic play area of the classroom into a dance area. Include a selection of dance outfits for both boys and girls and a variety of types of music. Listed below are suggestions for materials to include in a multicultural classroom dance area.

Dress-Up Clothes

- tutus made from stretch halters and netting
- colorful vests
- lapas (African skirts) made from 1 yard of African fabric; they are tied at the side
- silky shirts
- blazers
- hats, including top hats and crowns
- ballet and tap shoes
- shoes from many cultures, such as moccasins, Chinese sandals, and slippers from Pakistan

Accessories

- ▲ scarves
- ▲ ribbon streamers
- ▲ gloves
- ▲ Mardi Gras beads
- ▲ artificial flowers

Additional Items

- ▲ pictures of dancers from around the world
- ▲ mirrors
- ▲ stage made of hollow wooden blocks
- ▲ tickets

Music Recordings

- ▲ *The Nutcracker,* Tchaikovsky
- ▲ *Smilin' Island of Song,* Cedella Marley Booker
- ▲ *Africa: Drum, Chant and Instrumental Music*
- ▲ *Homrong,* Musicians of the National Dance Company of Cambodia

Integrated Curriculum Activities

Include the song and interactive chart "Dance Myself Dizzy" (activity 6.13).

There are many excellent diversity books that go with the dance unit. Examples are:

Color Dance, by Ann Jonas	multiracial, includes male dancer
Mimi's Tutu, by Tynia Thomassie	African American
Silent Lotus, by Jeanne M. Lee	Cambodian, main character is deaf
Lili on Stage, by Rachel Isadora	multiracial, includes male dancers
Lion Dancer, by Kate Waters and Madeline Sloveny-Low	Chinese American, includes male dancer
Song and Dance Man, by Karen Ackerman	intergenerational
Powwow, by George Ancona	Native American
Red Dancing Shoes, by Denise Lewis Patrick	African American
My Ballet Class, by Rachel Isadora	multiracial
Dance at Grandpa's, by Laura Ingalls Wilder	intergenerational

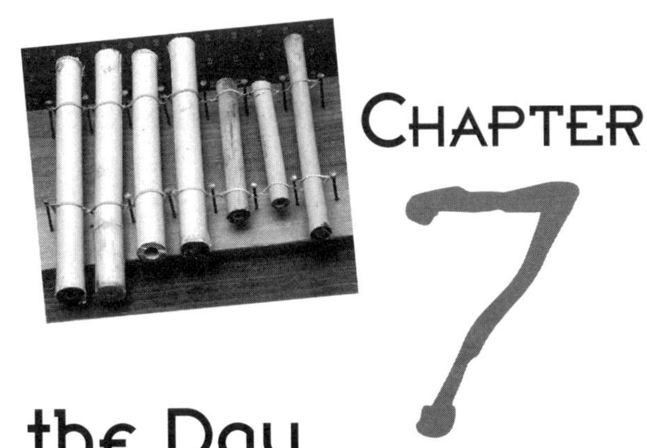

Chapter 7

Music Throughout the Day

A group of children arrived for their turn in a large-motor room only to find the room still occupied by another class. They were five minutes early. The children were bubbling with energy, and their teacher quickly sought a means to keep them calm and safe as they waited. She had the children sit down, and she began to sing a song about what each child wanted to do in the large-motor room. The song was made up on the spot to the tune of "Here We Go 'Round the Mulberry Bush." The children were intrigued by the song because it was about them. By the time the song was finished, the other class had left the room, and the new class could enter. The teacher had not only averted a difficult management situation but transformed it into a positive musical experience.

▲ ▲ ▲

Chanthyda was playing with dolls in the dramatic play area as her teacher changed the tape on the class tape recorder. As the music began to play, Chanthyda stopped playing and listened intently for a few moments. Then with a big smile on her face she announced, "That Cambodian music!" She had recognized the music of her culture.

▲ ▲ ▲

Opportunities for exploring music and the nature of sound surround children throughout the day. Teachers can capitalize on these teachable moments by observing children's interests as they interact with materials and with one another in the classroom. Teachers can develop a repertoire of songs to introduce as children work in various areas of the classroom and prepare for transitions.

Teachers' Questions

Why is it important to encourage music throughout the day?

Music is a natural part of children's lives and can enhance and extend other aspects of learning. Many teachers discover that singing quietly about an activity helps some children who are easily frustrated remain focused on the activity. Music also draws some children to an area of the classroom they might not typically visit. Singing is an excellent tool for calming anxious children and encouraging participation.

How can teachers use music in all areas of the classroom?

Teachers can make up songs spontaneously, perhaps by altering the words to familiar tunes. They can also plan specific songs to include during special activities or for particular areas of the classroom. Examples of both types of song are included in the activities in this chapter.

When should teachers introduce music activities?

Teachers should capitalize on teachable moments when they observe children experimenting with sound or movement. Teachers may also introduce music when they feel it will extend or encourage increased participation. For example, if several children have built a bus in the block area, the teacher might decide to sing "The Wheels on the Bus." The children would probably eagerly join in, and the song might extend their thinking about the parts of the bus. Other children might decide to become involved in the play.

The teacher does not spend all day singing. Classrooms are dynamic. Music emerges when the teachers and children feel it is appropriate.

How can teachers use music to facilitate transitions?

Singing calms down children and draws their attention. The words to songs can communicate to children what they will be doing next. Teachers can add children's names to songs, either a few at a time or singly, to move them to a new activity. Children waiting to be called are involved in listening to the song or singing along. Management difficulties that often accompany transitions with young children are largely avoided when teachers use songs to facilitate the process. Examples of transition songs are included in the activities in this chapter.

How do children respond to the inclusion of music throughout the day?

Children usually respond eagerly to music, often with a renewed interest in the activity at hand. Children sometimes seem more comfortable singing about an activity rather than talking about it. When children are a part of a classroom where spontaneous use of music is accepted and valued, many begin to create songs themselves as they engage in play. Music becomes yet another vehicle for expressing their creativity. Examples of three songs composed by preschool children during their play are included in activity 7.15.

Should teachers play background music during class?

Many teachers choose to include recorded music during free choice parts of the day. Some music is soothing to children and tends to calm the classroom. Soft music often creates a relaxing, friendly atmosphere that both children and parents find comforting.

Teachers can include recordings of music from many cultures as a backdrop for ongoing classroom activities. This broadens the musical perspectives of the entire class and can be very affirming for children who come from the cultures included on the recording.

What criteria should teachers use in selecting recordings?

Teachers should choose music that represents a variety of musical styles and cultures. While adults often assume that children will only enjoy recordings made for children, they actually relate readily to a wide range of music, from classical to jazz and from Taiwanese to Bolivian. If teachers rely solely on children's recordings, they deprive their class of the opportunity to experience this wealth of music.

Music used as a background for general classroom activities should be kept soft. Loud music can distract children rather than contribute to a relaxed atmosphere.

What should teachers do if children don't like a particular type of music?

Teachers should scaffold. In other words, they can guide children to listen for an aspect of the music that they may find interesting or feel more comfortable with. Musical styles that adults are unfamiliar with or music from cultures they have not experienced often sound harsh or dissonant to them. The same is true for children. While not every child or every adult will enjoy all music, scaffolding can help children relate to music they previously found strange by helping them focus on a particular aspect of the music. For example, when listening to West African music, the teacher might want to draw attention to the intriguing drum patterns. Children often find the drums exciting and then decide they like the music after all. Teachers often discover that over time children develop an appreciation and enjoyment for a wide range of music.

Suggestions for recordings to use throughout the day, along with scaffolding ideas, are included in activity 7.16. The list is by no means inclusive. It represents a range of possibilities for teachers to choose from.

Are there specific musical concepts that teachers can explore with children throughout the day?

Yes. Elements of sound such as loud and soft, fast and slow, and speeding up and slowing down occur in natural situations throughout the day. Teachers can use these experiences to help children draw relationships to the same concepts in music. Examples of classroom experiences that relate to musical concepts are listed in activity 7.17.

Music Activities for Throughout the Day

7.1 With Our Blocks

Sally Moomaw
© 1997

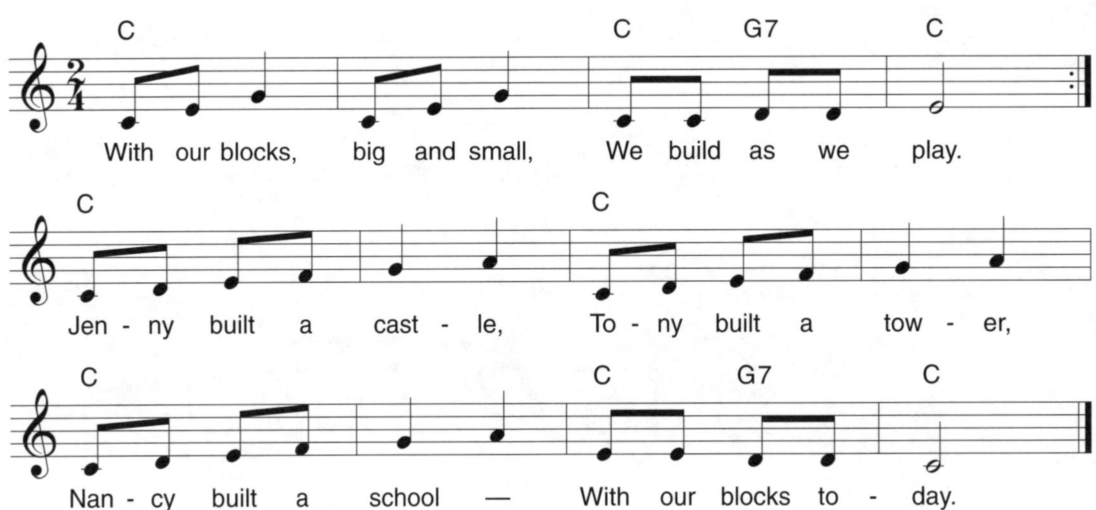

Curriculum Area—Blocks

Description

Children enjoy singing this song as they build. The singing often sparks additional interest in building and draws new children to the area.

Child's Level

This activity is appropriate for either preschool or kindergarten children.

Why Appropriate

Children can add words for their own block structures to the song.

Musical Extension

Children also like to sing this song at group time. They can play the beats on wood blocks to emphasize rhythm.

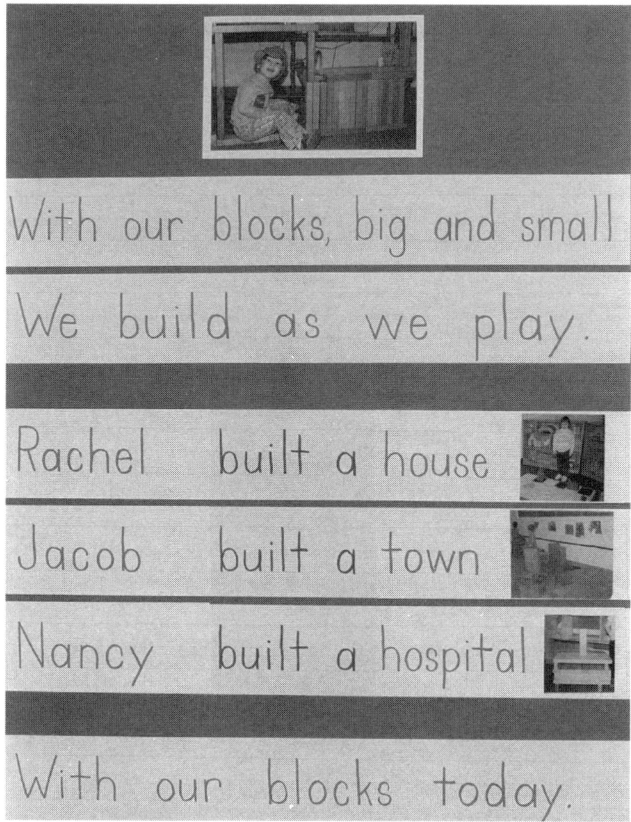

Whole-Language Extension

Materials

- ▲ red poster board (or color desired), 28 by 22 inches
- ▲ sentence strips
- ▲ photographs of the children's block structures

Description

Print the words to the song on sentence strips, as shown. The first line, which repeats in the song, is printed only once. Leave space for word cards showing the children's names and what they built. After the chart is laminated, attach pockets made from clear laminating film in the blank spaces. Make a word card for each child's block construction by mounting a photograph of it to a sentence strip and printing the child's label for the construction. Children can insert the word cards into the pockets on the chart. Some children may want to write the words themselves.

7.2 Butter Making

Diane Blackburn
Used by permission

Curriculum Area–Cooking

Description

Making butter is a popular cooking activity in preschool and kindergarten. To make butter, pour whipping cream into small containers, such as baby food jars, and close them tightly. Have the children shake the jars until the butter forms.

Child's Level

This song is appropriate for either preschool or kindergarten children.

Why Appropriate

Singing as they shake the jars helps children wait for the butter to form.

The words to the song reinforce in children's minds the procedure used to make the butter.

Musical Extension

Children can reenact the making of butter by shaking water maracas (activity 4.4) as they sing the song at group time.

7.3 Hammering

Sally Moomaw
© 1980

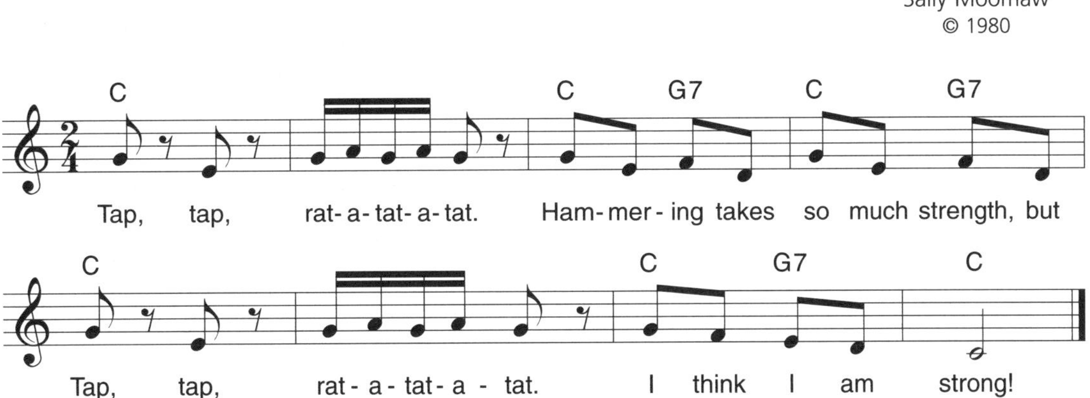

Curriculum Area—Woodworking

Description

You can introduce this song as children are engaged in woodworking. Add the names of the children hammering to the last line of the song; for example, "Sarah and Emily are strong."

Child's Level

This song is appropriate for either preschool or kindergarten children.

Why Appropriate

Children enjoy woodworking, but hammering a nail all the way into the wood requires perseverance. The song encourages children to continue the activity.

Hammering creates a natural rhythm, which is reinforced in the song.

Musical Extension

Children can play wood blocks to imitate hammering as they sing the song at group time.

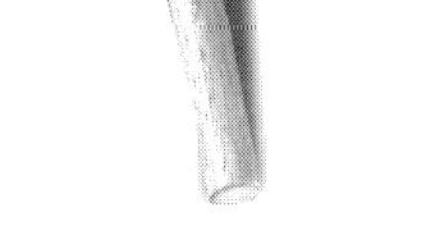

7.4 Snip, Snip, Snip

(Inclusion Activity)

words by Sally Moomaw
Traditional tune

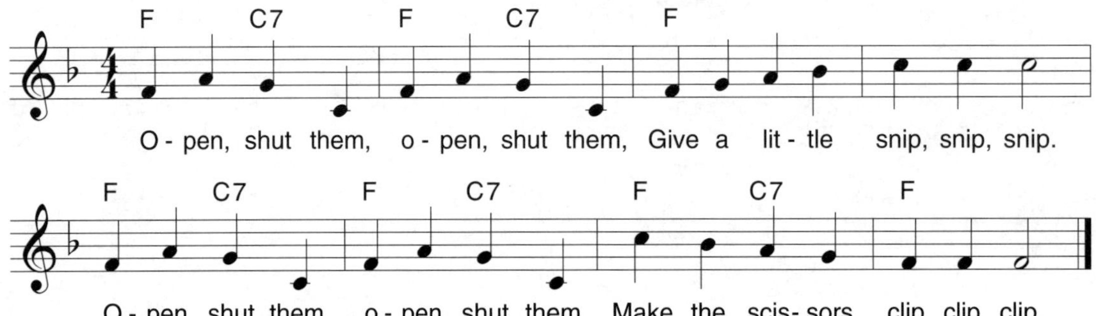

Curriculum Area—Art

Description

Some children have difficulty opening and closing scissors. Children with motor delays often find cutting to be especially challenging. This song, adapted from the familiar finger play "Open, Shut Them," reminds children of the motion required when cutting with scissors. Singing as children work with the scissors seems to relax those who are experiencing difficulties and to encourage them to keep trying.

Child's Level

This activity is appropriate for either preschool or kindergarten children, especially for special situations such as those described above.

Why Appropriate

The words fit the movements required to work scissors.

The song reminds children of the motions needed to work scissors. Singing is sometimes less intrusive than telling.

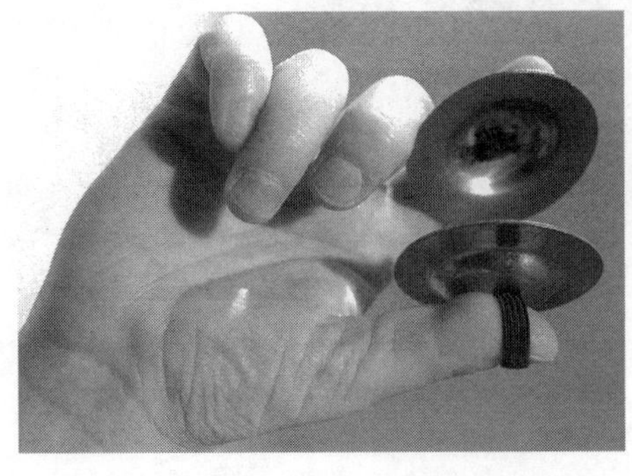

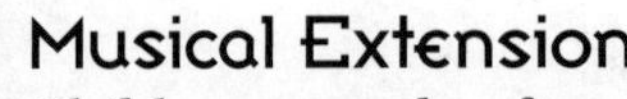

Musical Extension

Children can play finger cymbals or castanets with one hand as they sing both versions of the song. One finger cymbal or castanet fits over the thumb and the other over an opposing finger. Children are thus again practicing the open and shut movement of scissors.

7.5 Throw That Ball

Tina Costanzo
Used by permission

Curriculum Area—Gross Motor

Description

This song seems to heighten the pleasure children experience in playing catch. Less active children are frequently drawn into the game.

Child's Level

This activity is appropriate for preschool or kindergarten children.

Why Appropriate

Children respond eagerly to having their names added to the song.

The words can be changed to encourage a variety of ball activities.

7.6 Jump Myself Jiggly

words by Sally Moomaw
music by Peter Moomaw
Used by permission

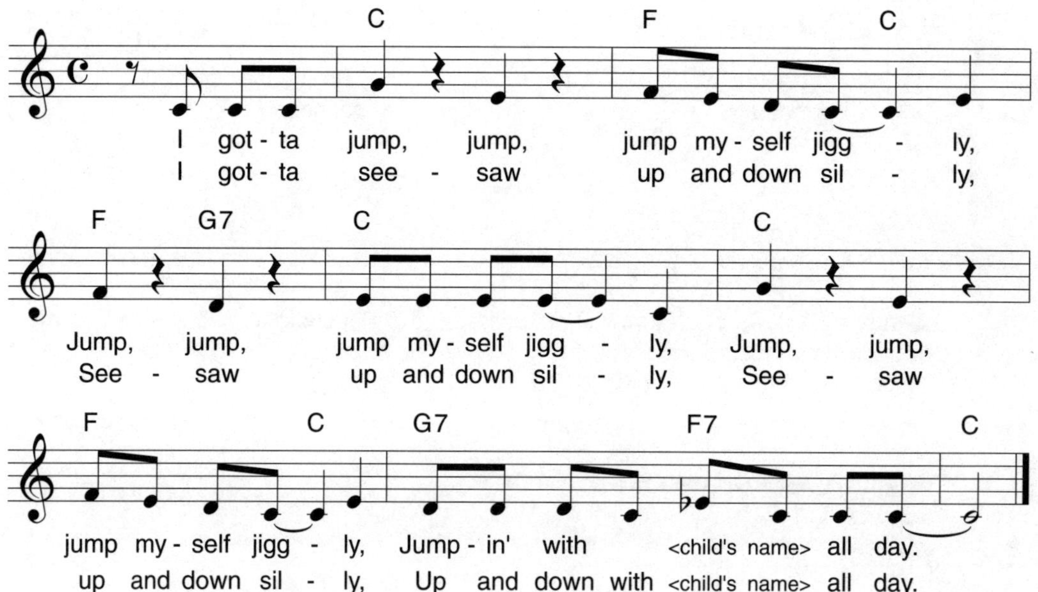

Curriculum Area–Gross Motor

Description

This is an adaptation of the song "Dance Myself Dizzy" (activity 6.13). Alter the words to fit the activities of the children. Hearing the song is an enticement for many children to join in the play.

Child's Level

This activity is appropriate for either preschool or kindergarten children.

Why Appropriate

The song encourages gross-motor activity.

7.7 Where, Oh Where?

(Transition Song)

words by Sally Moomaw
Tune adapted from "Paw Paw Patch"
Lyrics © 1979, 1996

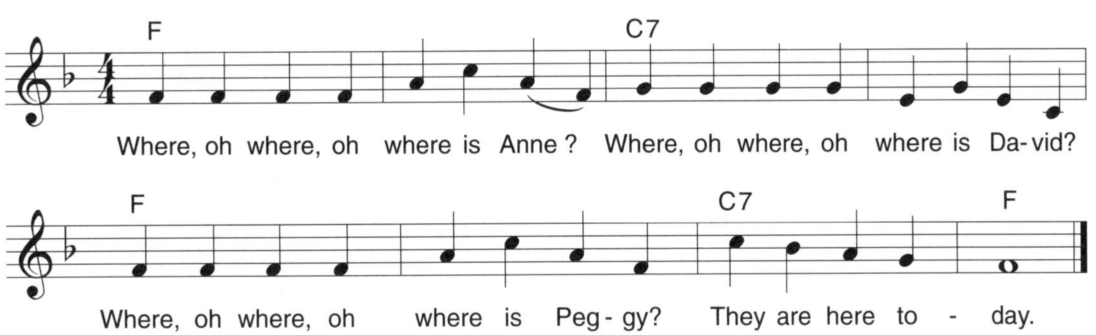

Description

You can use this song to transition children into group time. It is also a good welcoming song.

Child's Level

This song is appropriate for either preschool or kindergarten children.

Whole-Language Extension

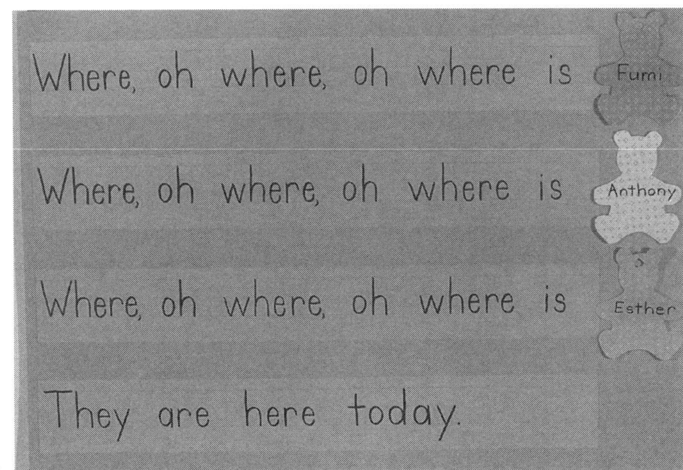

Materials

- ▲ pink poster board (or color desired), 28 by 20 inches
- ▲ bear cut-outs from wallpaper
- ▲ sentence strips

Description

Write the words to the song on sentence strips and mount them to the poster board. Leave a space at the end of lines one through three to hang a bear. Print each child's name on a bear cut-out. Laminate the chart and the bears. Use magnetic tape, Velcro, or a paper fastener to hang the bears on the chart.

7.8 I Have a Friend

(Transition Song)

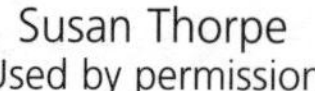

I have a friend whose name is Da- vid sit- ting right next to my friend A- my,

sit- ting right next to my friend Jes - se, put - ting their mats a - away.
wash- ing their hands for lunch.

Description

You can use this song to transition children away from group activities.

Child's Level

This song is appropriate for either preschool or kindergarten children.

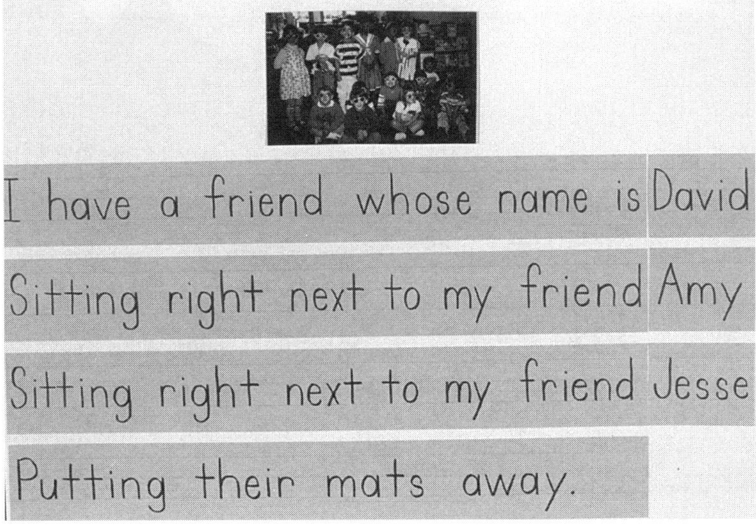

Whole-Language Extension

Materials

- ▲ poster board, 28 by 22 inches
- ▲ sentence strips
- ▲ class photo or picture of children

Description

Write the words to the song on sentence strips, and mount the strips and the class photo to the poster board. Write each child's name on an 8-inch piece of sentence strip. Laminate the chart and the name cards. Use magnetic tape, Velcro, or a paper fastener to hang the name cards on the chart.

7.9 Put on Our Socks

(Transition Song)

Sally Moomaw
© 1980

Description

You can sing this song as you help children dress prior to going outside.

Child's Level

This song is appropriate for toddlers or young preschoolers due to its short length.

Modification

Alter the words to suit the occasion. For example, you might sing, "Put on our coats, put on our hats. . . ."

7.10 What Will You Do?

(Transition Song)

words by Sally Moomaw
Tune adapted from "Skip to My Lou"
© 1982, 1996

Description

You can use this song to transition children to a new area, such as outside.

Child's Level

This song is appropriate for either preschool or kindergarten children.

Modification

Change the words of the last phrase to suit your needs. For example: "When you go home from school today . . . ," "When you come back to school tomorrow . . . ," or "When you go to the gym today. . . ."

7.11 Look at What We're Wearing (Transition Song)

Sally Moomaw
© 1982, 1996

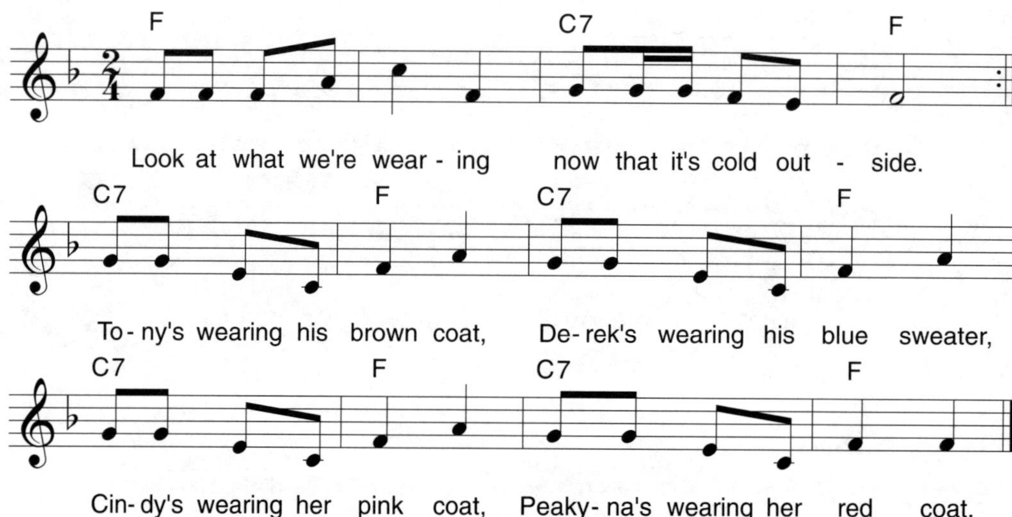

Description

You can use this song for transitioning children outside. The song reinforces color words and articles of clothing.

Child's Level

This song is appropriate for preschool or kindergarten children.

Modification

Change the words to reflect the season of the year.

7.12 Everybody Have a Seat

(Transition Song)

words by Sally Moomaw
Traditional tune, "Shortnin' Bread"

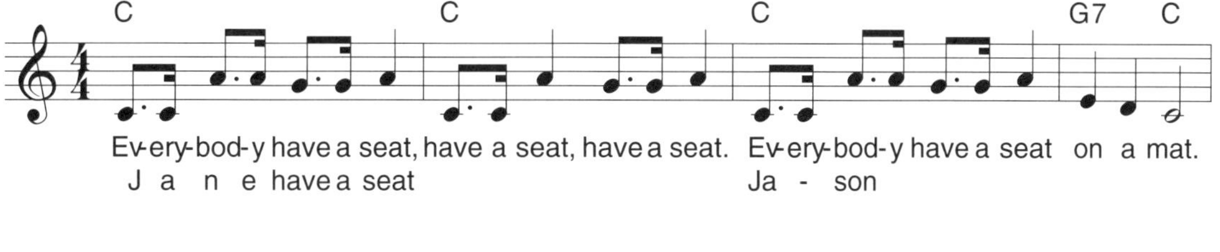

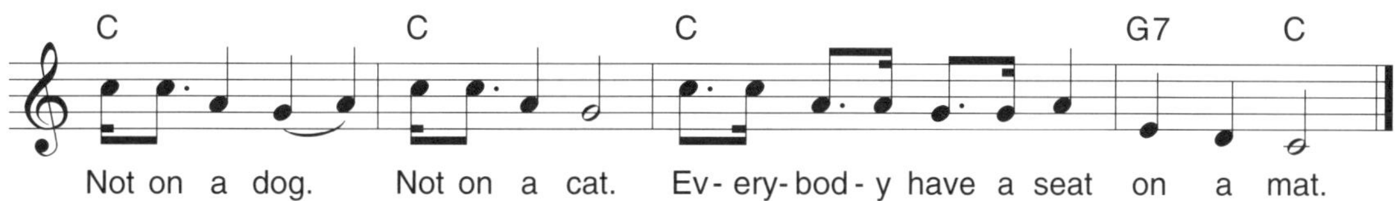

Description

You can use this song to help move children from various areas of the classroom to a group time area.

Child's Level

This song is most appropriate for older preschool or kindergarten children who understand and enjoy the humor of the rhyming words.

Modification

Change the words to fit your classroom. For example, if children sit on the floor, they could sing:

> Everybody have a seat on the floor.
> Not on the windows. Not on the door...

If the children are to move to chairs, the song could say:

> Everybody have a seat on your chair.
> Not on a horsy. Not on a bear...

7.13 If Your Name Begins

(Transition Song)

Mary Ann McPherson
Used by permission

Description

This song helps children focus on the beginning letters of their names and the names of the other children in the class. They begin to draw the relationship between the letter and the sound it makes. You can hold up the letters as you sing this song.

Child's Level

This song is most appropriate for older preschool and kindergarten children.

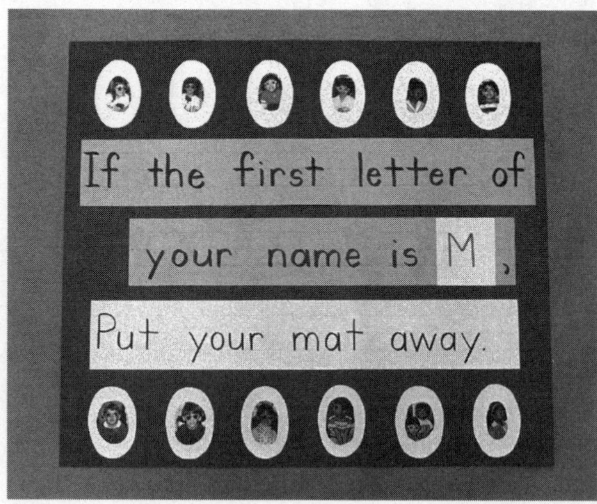

Whole-Language Extension

Materials

- ▲ poster board, 22 by 19 inches
- ▲ sentence strips
- ▲ photographs of the children
- ▲ index cards

Description

Write the words to the song on sentence strips and attach them to the board with rubber cement. Mount children's photographs around the border of the chart. Laminate. Use magnetic tape, Velcro, or a paper fastener to hang index cards with the necessary letters on the chart.

7.14 Field Trip Song

(Transition Song)

words by Sally Moomaw
Traditional tune, "London Bridge"

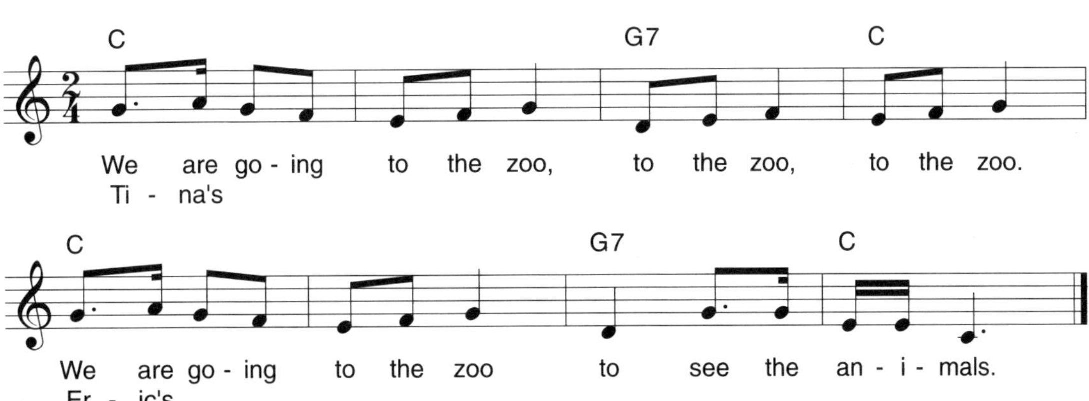

Description

This song helps children prepare for upcoming field trips. You can use it as a transition song to assemble children prior to leaving.

Child's Level

This song is appropriate for preschool or kindergarten children.

Modification

Change the words to fit any field trip destination. For example:

> We are going to the library
> To choose some books.

7.15 Children's Songs

Description

These songs were created by preschool children engaged in activities in their classrooms.

Joseph made up this song as he worked at the woodworking table:

Joseph De Marco
Used by permission

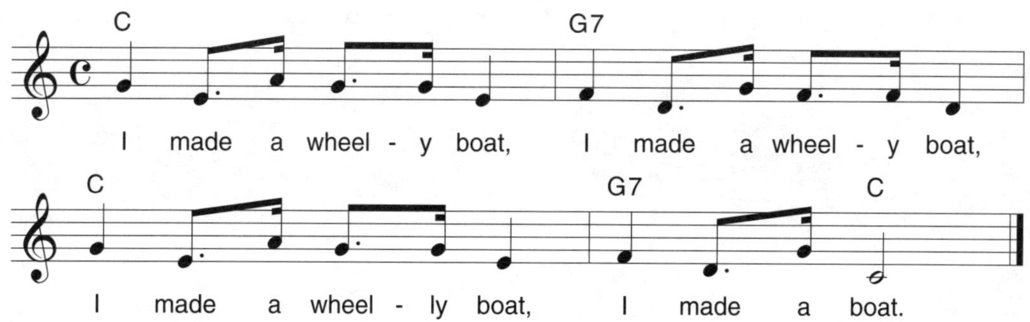

Emily created this song as she looked at a snowflake shape she had cut from paper in an open art area:

Emily Kamholtz
Used by permission

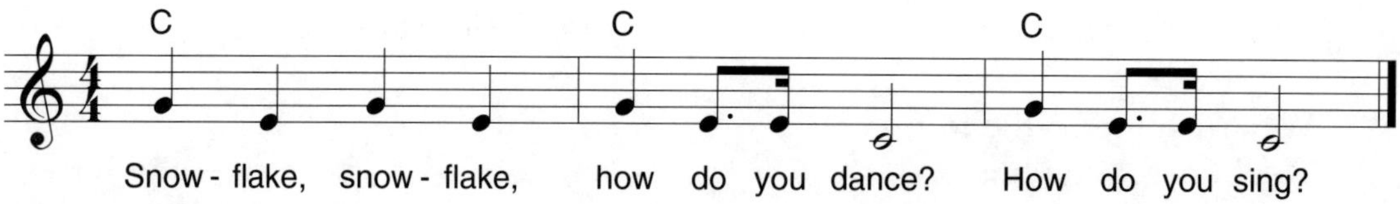

Peter sang this song (to the tune of "Here We Go 'Round the Mulberry Bush") to accompany a train he was creating with blocks:

Peter Moomaw
Used by permission

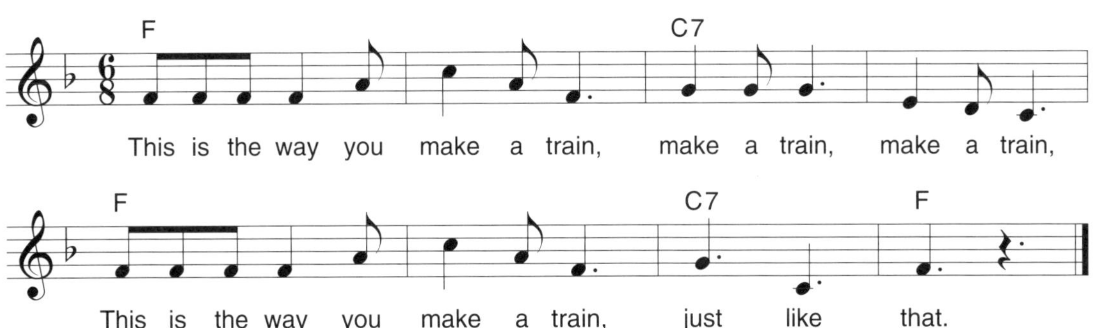

First you put the engine on,
Engine on, engine on,
First you put the engine on,
Just like that.

Then you put the hopper on...

Then you put the boxcar on...

Then you put the caboose on...

7.16 Listening Guide to Music of Diverse Cultures

Recording
Africa: Drum, Chant, and Instrumental Music

Culture
Niger, Mali, and Upper Volta

Scaffolding
Direct children's attention to the excitement of the repeating drum patterns.

Recording
The World Sings Goodnight

Culture
Thirty-three different cultures sing lullabies in their native tongues

Scaffolding
Let the children guess whether father, mother, grandmother, or grandfather is singing to their little one.

Recording
D is for Dulcimer—Glenn Morgan

Culture
Irish, Scottish, Appalachian

Scaffolding
Children seem immediately comfortable with the sounds of the hammered dulcimer, so scaffolding is not necessary.

Recording
Dream Catcher—Kevin Locke (Tokeya Inajin)

Culture
Native American—Lakota

Scaffolding
This tape has a quiet, soothing sound. Nature sounds are incorporated along with the cedar flute. Ask the children what part of nature the flute music might represent.

Recording
Homrong—Musicians of the National Dance Company of Cambodia

Culture
Cambodian

Scaffolding
The *chappay* (a string instrument) is prominent in this recording. Ask the children if they have heard any other instruments with strings. Children often find the voice qualities and wind instruments strange to their ears. Try directing their attention at first to the drum, which is more familiar.

Recording
How the West Was Lost—Peter Kater with R. Carlos Nakai

Culture
Euro-American and Native American

Scaffolding
This recording combines Native American flute with such Western instruments as piano, oboe, and cello. This very soothing music will help calm even the most hectic day in the classroom.

Recording
The Oud—H. Aram Gulezyan

Culture
Near and Middle East

Scaffolding
The *oud* became known as the *lute* in Western culture. Children quickly relate its sound to the more familiar guitar. This melodious tape introduces them to Eastern melodies.

Recording
United Tribes International Powwow

Culture
Native American

Scaffolding
Powwow music may sound unusual to children's ears. Consistent throughout powwow music is the steady beat of the drum, which represents the heartbeat of Mother Earth. Help children focus on this drumbeat and relate it to their own heartbeats.

Recording
Drums & Voices of Korea—Samul-Nori

Culture
Korean

Scaffolding
Four native Korean instruments (large and small gong, round drum, and hourglass shaped drum) dominate this recording, along with the singing. Direct the children's attention to the excitement produced by these instruments.

Recording
Japan: Traditional Vocal & Instrumental Music—Ensemble Nipponia

Culture
Japanese

Scaffolding
Several traditional Japanese instruments are featured on this recording. The *shakuhachi*, a bamboo flute, is very soothing. The *shamisen* sounds similar to a banjo, while the *biwa* is more guitar-like. As the children listen to these instruments, ask if they have heard any other instruments that sound similar.

Recording
Smilin' Island of Song—Cedella Marley Booker

Culture
Jamaican (Reggae)

Scaffolding
The repetition of melody and words along with the relaxing reggae style is appealing to young children, so scaffolding is not necessary.

Recording
Quinchuquimanda: Music of the Andes—Karullacta

Culture
Andean (Ecuador, Peru, Bolivia)

Scaffolding
Much of this music sounds happy, upbeat, and easy for children to listen to. Direct attention to the indigenous instruments, such as the bamboo pipes or strummed *charango*, which have a familiar sound.

7.17 Music Concepts Throughout the Day

Concept	Guided Observations
pitch	Direct children's attention to the chirping of a bird and the barking of a dog. Ask them to decide which animal has a higher voice.
pitch	Listen to a siren as it approaches and moves away. Ask children if they can imitate the sound as it goes up and down.
beat	Direct children's attention to the ticking of a clock. Inexpensive wind-up travel clocks tick loudly. Children can also hold them close to their ears.
rhythm	Listen with children to the patterns of sound that rain makes as it hits the roof.
rhythm	Encourage children to compare the sound of feet walking with the sound of feet skipping.
rhythm	Listen for rhythm in things that move, such as the squeak of a water wheel in the sensory table or the thump of a teeter-totter as it hits the ground.
accelerando	Have children close their eyes and listen to a bouncing ball. It starts slowly and speeds up as it bounces closer and closer to the ground.
dynamics	Compare the sound of voices in your classroom with voices coming from other classrooms.

Concept	Guided Observations
tempo	Compare the sounds of children walking with the sound of adults walking. Children's steps are much quicker.
timbre	Direct children's attention to the sound a hammer makes when it hits a nail and when it hits wood.
timbre, dynamics	Compare the sound of children's feet on pavement and in the grass; on linoleum and on carpet.
dynamics	Listen with the children and list sounds they hear that are loud and sounds they identify as soft.
timbre	On breezy days, listen to the wind in the trees. Ask children if they can think of an instrument that sounds similar.

Group Times

A preschool class had just finished singing the song "No Witches." Alice suddenly announced, "The song is a pattern. See? The first and third lines are the same and the second and fourth lines are the same. It's a pattern!" Alice had recognized the form of the song. The melody did indeed form an alternating pattern.

▲ ▲ ▲

Group music experiences give children the opportunity to create music collaboratively and share ideas. The group time activities are often coordinated with a whole-language activity, such as an interactive chart or a big book, or a whole-math activity, such as estimation or patterning. Music helps teachers pace group-time experiences and maintain children's focus.

Teachers' Questions

Why are group music activities important?

Through group music experiences children construct important relationships about music. For example:

Singing in Tune—Children must hear the pitches others are singing and then attempt to produce matching pitches themselves.

Staying Together—Children learn to regulate their rate of singing to that of the group.

Form—Children discover that some lines of music sound the same and some sound different. Some children, like Alice, realize that this is a pattern.

Rhythm—Children develop a feel for the beat and may begin to hear and reproduce rhythmic patterns.

What factors should teachers consider when planning music groups?

Teachers should consider the ages and experiences of the children. This will help determine the length and complexity of the activities as well as the length of the group time. Toddlers need activities that involve them directly, such as songs with their names or specific movements. Preschool and kindergarten children respond eagerly to music activities that correlate with specific subjects of interest, such as snow, or the overall curriculum. Music thus helps reinforce other areas of learning.

What types of activities should be included in group times?

Teachers should provide a variety of musical experiences, including songs, rhythm activities, instruments, movement, and listening. The entire group time does not need to be music. Often teachers include stories, whole-language activities, or math activities. Music helps pace the group time so children more easily remain focused.

How many activities should be included?

Five or six is typical. Toddler activities are very short, so five or six activities usually take about five minutes. Activities for preschool children are a bit longer. Six activities might take 10 to 15 minutes. The length and complexity of activities for kindergarten children expand as do their attention spans. Six kindergarten activities could take 20 minutes or more. The teacher monitors the pacing of the group and can extend or cut back on activities as needed.

What should teachers consider when arranging the sequence of activities?

Pacing is important for maintaining the attention of the group and avoiding management problems. When planning the sequence of activities, it is important to alternate quiet and active activities. This keeps children from becoming overstimulated and helps them maintain concentration. Quiet activities include singing, clapping rhythms, chanting, and listening. Movement and playing instruments are more active.

What is a good way to begin the group?

Beginning with a familiar song allows children to join in immediately and helps focus their attention. Often transition songs are used. Hearing their names quickly draws children's attention. After the opening song, the teacher can introduce a new activity that requires closer concentration.

What is a good way to end the group?

The group time should end as it began, with a quiet song to calm the children before they move to their next activity or prepare to go home. Transition songs are effective for ending group times because children can be called a few at a time to leave the group. This avoids the management problems that can occur when everyone moves at once.

Should everyone come to group time?

The answer depends on the age of the children and the philosophy of the teacher or school. Toddlers are much too young for a required group time. However, they typically love music and most come eagerly when they hear it begin. Preschool teachers vary on whether they choose to have everyone come to group time or not. Some teachers allow children to choose either group time or one other quiet area of the room. Many teachers find that after a few days all of the children want to be part of the group time. Kindergartens typically have some group experiences for everyone.

How can teachers plan longitudinally for music activities?

Most music activities will become progressively longer and more challenging during the year. Children's understanding of musical concepts continues to develop over a long period of time. They need repeated opportunities to participate in activities that gradually increase in complexity.

The teacher should sequence changes carefully so that they follow a natural progression from easy to more difficult. For example, rhythm might start with the simple clapping of names at the beginning of the year. Then instruments could be added to replace the clapping. Toward the end of the year, children might be ready to combine rhythmic patterns to accompany a chant or song. Such longitudinal planning ensures successful learning experiences for children.

How long should teachers continue specific songs or activities?

Children need repeated experiences in order to learn songs and rhythms well and explore musical extensions. Activities should be repeated for several consecutive days, perhaps with slight alterations each day. For example, the children might sing a song the first day, clap the beats as they sing it the second day, and add instruments the third day. The activity should be repeated periodically over several weeks so that children can remember it. Children enjoy repeating familiar songs throughout the year.

Sample Lesson Plans

8.1 All About Us

Sample Lesson Plan for Two Year Olds

	Area	Activity	Why Selected
1.	transition song	"Where Is Jeffrey?"	very short melody easy to sing uses each child's name
2.	rhythm	Clap children's names	beginning rhythm activity uses children's own names
3.	instruments, song	"Hear Our Jingle Bells" (children accompany song with jingle bells)	short song with simple melody and words jingle bells easy to play and fit words of song
4.	listening, musical concept (timbre)	listening game (wood block and bells)	instruments have easily distinguishable differences in sound
5.	movement	"Step, Step, Step"—children follow directions in song	short, simple song directions easy to follow movements easy enough for two year olds
6.	transition song	"Put on Our Coats"	short song with simple melody and words helps children prepare for next activity

Description of Activities

Activity 1

Add the name of each child to the very simple song "Where Is Jeffrey?" The teacher can pretend not to see the child at first in a "peek-a-boo" fashion. Toddlers readily respond.

Activity 2

Children can join in as the teacher claps each child's name several times.

Activity 3

For this activity, children accompany "Hear Our Jingle Bells" (activity 4.6) with jingle bells. Each child will need an instrument. Include each child's name in the song. With older children, the activity would begin with everyone singing the song and clapping the beats. Two year olds, however, may have difficulty waiting for the instruments, so pass out the bells at the beginning of the activity.

Activity 4

In this listening game, show the children a wood block and jingle bells and play each one. Play the two instruments behind a screen and let the children guess which one they hear.

Activity 5

Sing "Step, Step, Step" (activity 6.2) and have the children join you with the movements.

Activity 6

For this transition song, sing "Put On Our Coats" (variant of activity 7.9) as the children prepare to go outside. If desired, add each child's name to the beginning of the song. For example:

8.2 Wake Up

Sample Lesson Plan for Two Year Olds

	Area	Activity	Why Selected
1.	transition song	"Where, Oh Where?"	short and easy to sing uses each child's name
2.	song, movement	"Rockabye, Lullaby"	short song with simple melody and words swaying movements easy and natural for toddlers
3.	musical concept (loud/soft), listening	children listen to a quiet maraca and "wake up" when it gets loud	loud and soft easy to distinguish logical follow-up to previous activity
4.	instruments, musical concept (loud/soft), song	children play loud and soft on maracas according to the words of the song	song reinforces previous activity provides concrete experience in creating dynamics short song with simple melody and words
5.	movement	"Stretching"	short, simple song directions easy to follow movements easy and natural for toddlers
6.	rhythm, transition chant	"Who Can Play?" (children clap with the teacher)	short chant with strong beats helps children prepare for next activity

Description of Activities

Activity 1

Add the name of each child to "Where, Oh Where?" (activity 7.7) to provide individual attention within a group experience. Hearing their names encourages children to join in.

Activity 2

Children can join in when they feel ready as you sing "Rockabye, Lullaby" (activity 2.1). Often children pretend to rock their teddy bears back and forth to the music and end by lying down and preparing to sleep.

Activity 3

This activity is a follow-up game to activity 2. Play a maraca very softly as the children pretend to sleep. When the maraca gets loud, they wake up.

Activity 4

Children play maracas or baby rattles along with the song "Playing Maracas." At the end of each line, they play loud or soft sounds with the maracas, depending on the words. Each child will need an instrument.

Sally Moomaw
© 1996

Activity 5

Children imitate the movements in the song "Stretching" (activity 6.1) as they join in with the teacher.

Activity 6

Children can clap with you as you chant and clap the beats to "Who Can Play?" (activity 3.4). Add each child's name. If desired, children can transition to the next activity when they hear their names.

8.3 Animals

Sample Lesson Plan for Two Year Olds

	Area	Activity	Why Selected
1.	transition song	"Where Is Jeffrey?" adaptation	helps children focus on a new activity short and easy to sing uses each child's name
2.	song, instruments	"Swish, Swish, Swish" (children use water maracas to accompany song)	easy to sing water maracas are simple for young children to play
3.	rhythm	clap names of familiar animals	good beginning rhythm activity clapping is a favorite activity of young children
4.	song	"Birdie"	very short melody is easy for young children to sing children have seen birds many times
5.	movement	children dramatize birds flying and walking	children have had opportunities to observe birds
6.	transition song	"Do You See"	uses each child's name builds vocabulary

Description of Activities

Activity 1

This song is an adaptation of the song "Where Is Jeffrey?" (activity 8.1). Change the words to, "I See Jeffrey, I See Jeffrey, in his red shirt, in his red shirt." Add each child's name to the song.

Activity 2

For this age group, sing just the first verse of "Swish, Swish, Swish" (activity 2.15). Children can play water maracas as they sing. You might wish to include a small plastic fish in each maraca when you make them.

Activity 3

Clap the syllables of animal words as you show pictures of animals that are familiar to the children. Children can join in by clapping in their own way. (See activity 3.2 for a similar example.)

Activity 4

Sing the song "Birdie" (activity 2.2) several times. The children will join in when ready.

Activity 5

In this movement activity, children pretend to be birds flying, hopping, and sitting in their nests. Continue to sing the "Birdie" song as the children move like birds, if desired.

Activity 6

This song is sung to the last two lines of the traditional song, "The Muffin Man."

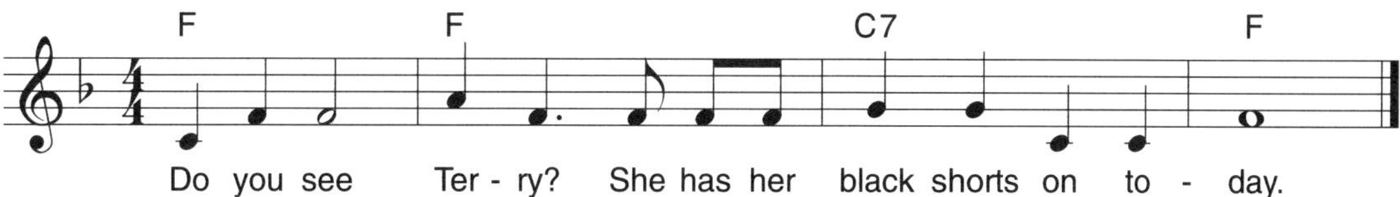

8.4 Autumn

Sample Lesson Plan for Three to Four Year Olds

	Area	Activity	Why Selected
1.	song	"Autumn Leaves"	song is short, repetitive, and easy to sing relevant to time of year children can add their ideas to the song
2.	song, math extension	"3 Little Bats"	song is short and easy to sing coordinates with interactive whole-language and math chart
3.	musical concept (fast/slow)	children watch and compare a leaf and nut falling	preparation for movement activity relates to fast and slow in movement and music
4.	movement	children dramatize falling like a leaf and falling like a nut	allows children to experience and focus on fast and slow movements with their bodies relates to autumn season
5.	song, movement, math extension	"5 Brown Acorns"	relevant to season of year children can dramatize the words children can visualize repeated subtraction by 1
6.	transition song	"Shiver, Brrr"	children's names can be added to the song helps move children to the next activity relates to weather changes in autumn

Description of Activities

Activity 1

Children can suggest colors to add to the song "Autumn Leaves" (activity 2.5) as they sing along.

Activity 2

As children sing "3 Little Bats" (activity 2.4), they can help the teacher decide how many bats to put on each branch of the tree on the interactive chart.

Activity 3

Children can watch a leaf and a nut fall and describe the differences.

Activity 4

After they have observed the leaf and nut fall, children can use body movements to dramatize the action.

Activity 5

Each child has 5 acorn finger puppets to use as they reenact the song "5 Brown Acorns" (activity 6.8). They can remove one acorn for each verse and visualize the result.

Activity 6

The song "Shiver, Brrr" (activity 4.3) can be used as a transition song by changing the words to line three. For example:

> Nicholas, zip your coat up and keep it closed.

8.5 Winter

Sample Lesson Plan for Three to Four Year Olds

	Area	Activity	Why Selected
1.	transition song	"Where, Oh Where?"	helps children transition to group each child's name can be used in the song
2.	song, instruments, rhythm	"Snow Boy, Snow Girl" (children play finger cymbals to accompany song)	song is short and easy to sing finger cymbals add tone color
3.	movement, math extension, rhythm	"5 Little Snowmen"	chant has strong beat children can quantify each time a snowman is removed and visualize the subtraction
4.	movement, song	"Soft White Snowflakes"	children have had experiences with snowflakes relates to winter season song is easy to sing
5.	song, whole-language extension	"It Was Snow" with big book	song is short and easy to sing relates to season of year
6.	transition song	"Look at What We're Wearing"	helps children transition to new activity each child can be included in the song relates to winter theme

Description of Activities

Activity 1

Teachers can use the song “Where, Oh Where?” (activity 7.7) to help children transition into group time.

Activity 2

Children can clap the beats as they sing “Snow Boy, Snow Girl.” Then they can substitute finger cymbals for the claps (see activity 4.5).

Activity 3

Snowmen finger puppets make excellent props for children to use to dramatize the poem “5 Little Snowmen” (activity 3.10). Each time a snowman is removed, encourage the class to figure out how many are left. Fingers can be used in lieu of finger puppets.

Activity 4

After children have sung “Soft White Snowflakes,” they can use body movements to dramatize the snowflakes (activity 6.6).

Activity 5

Teachers can sing “It Was Snow” (activity 2.6) with the children as they point to the words in the big book.

Activity 6

“Look at What We’re Wearing” (activity 7.11) helps children prepare to transition to outside. Sing about what each child will wear.

8.6 Zoo

Sample Lesson Plan for Three to Four Year Olds

	Area	Activity	Why Selected
1.	song, whole-language extension	"The Hippopotamus" with big book	descriptive words children can read along with the big book as they sing
2.	movement	"The Hippopotamus"	descriptive words lend themselves well to dramatization relates to zoo theme
3.	rhythm, instruments	play zoo animal names on wood blocks	zoo animal names provide interesting rhythmic patterns children can contribute ideas of animal names to add
4.	rhythm	"Monkeys"	chant has a strong beat relates to familiar book, *Caps for Sale*
5.	math	estimate the number of monkeys in a jar	coordinates with previous activity encourages numerical thinking
6.	listening	listen to zoo animal sounds and attempt to identify the animals	focuses on listening preparation for upcoming field trip
7.	transition song	"We Are Going to the Zoo"	preparation for field trip each child's name can be added to song

Description of Activities

Activity 1

Children can follow along with the big book as they sing the words to "The Hippopotamus" (activity 6.7).

Activity 2

As the teacher sings "The Hippopotamus," the children can act out the words.

Activity 3

Children can name zoo animals and clap the syllables in the names. After they have clapped several names, substitute wood blocks for the clapping. Children can suggest zoo animals to add to the activity (activity 4.1).

Activity 4

For this activity, children can clap the beats as they recite the chant "Monkeys, Monkeys" (activity 3.5). They can suggest colors for the monkey's caps.

Activity 5

Children can estimate the number of tiny monkeys in a clear plastic jar.

Activity 6

Play a recording of animal sounds for the children to identify.

Activity 7

Add each child's name to the transition song "We Are Going to the Zoo" (activity 7.14) as they prepare to leave group time. The song is good preparation for an upcoming field trip.

8.7 Friends

Sample Lesson Plan for Four to Five Year Olds

	Area	Activity	Why Selected
1.	transition song	"It's So Good"	builds positive self-esteem each child's name can be added to the song
2.	rhythm, instruments	clap ***friend*** in other languages; add wood blocks	multicultural children are interested in exploring other languages
3.	literature	*My Friend,* by Taro Gomi	predictable book relates to topic of friendship
4.	movement	children dramatize the animals and actions in the book *My Friend*	literature extension
5.	song, whole-language extension, rhythm	"Bingo, Revisited"	reinforces each child's self-esteem and the unity of the group helps children focus on similarities and differences of names
6.	transition song	"I Have a Friend"	emphasizes friendship and feeling for the group each child's name can be added prepares children for next activity

Description of Activities

Activity 1
Sing each child's name in the transition song "It's So Good" (activity 4.11).

Activity 2
Say the word for *friend* in various languages and clap the rhythm of the words (activity 3.3).

Activity 3
My Friend, by Taro Gomi, is predictable and emphasizes what we can learn from animals. It sets the stage for the following movement activity.

Activity 4
Children can imitate the animals they have just heard about in *My Friend*.

Activity 5
Add each child's name to "Bingo, Revisited" (activity 2.11) and spell it on the chart. Children can clap the rhythm of the letters in the song.

Activity 6
"I Have a Friend" (activity 7.8) includes each child's name and reinforces the concept of friendship. It can be used to transition children to the next activity.

8.8 Dance

Sample Lesson Plan for Four to Five Year Olds

	Area	Activity	Why Selected
1.	transition song	"Everybody Have a Seat"	helps transition children into group time children's names can be added, if desired
2.	literature	*Color Dance,* by Ann Jonas	predictable book provides springboard for movement
3.	song, movement	"Rainbows of Color" (children dance with scarves)	enables children to act out the *Color Dance* book
4.	rhythm	children clap the names of the colors created by the scarves	coordinates with *Color Dance* helps children hear rhythmic patterns
5.	song, whole-language extension	"Dance Myself Dizzy" with interactive chart	children can read along on the interactive chart as they sing the song children can suggest colors to add to the song melody repeats and is easy to sing
6.	transition song	"Dance Myself Dizzy" adaptation	children's names can be added to the song

Description of Activities

Activity 1

Children enjoy the silly rhyming words in the transition song "Everybody Have a Seat" (activity 7.12). Teachers can add children's names to help draw them into group time.

Activity 2

Color Dance, by Ann Jonas, provides the foundation for the following movement activity. Children are intrigued by the colors created as the scarves mix together.

Activity 3

The song "Rainbows of Color" (activity 6.14) coordinates with *Color Dance*. After singing the song, children can dance with the scarves as they continue singing.

Activity 4

This activity provides children with another opportunity to explore color mixing. They can predict what new color will be created when two colors mix, watch as the teacher combines two colors of scarves, and clap the rhythm of the resulting color (as in activities, 3.1, 3.2, and 3.3).

Activity 5

Point to the words of the song on the chart as the children sing along (activity 6.13). Children can suggest color words to add to the chart.

Activity 6

This transition song is an adaptation of the previous song, "Dance Myself Dizzy." Change the last line to include the children's names, if desired. For example: "Dancin' with Peter all day."

8.9 Pizza

Sample Lesson Plan for Four to Five Year Olds

	Area	Activity	Why Selected
1.	transition song	"Everybody Come to Group"	helps children transition to group time children's names can be added to the song
2.	literature, song	"Lady with the Alligator Purse"	children love this silly song coordinates with pizza topic
3.	rhythm, instruments	"Pizza is Yummy" (children clap beats and then play beats with triangles)	simple chant with a strong beat children's names and ideas can be included in the chant
4.	rhythm, math extension	pizza patterns	clapping the rhythm created by the patterns helps reinforce patterning concepts coordinates with pizza theme
5.	rhythm	"Pizza Combo"	provides a more complex rhythm activity for older children
6.	transition song	"We Are Going to the Pizza Parlor"	prepares children for upcoming field trip helps transition children out of group time

Description of Activities

Activity 1

This transition song is sung to the tune of "London Bridge."

> Everybody come to group, come to group, come to group,
> Everybody come to group, We're singing about pizza today.
>
> Tina and Holly come to group, come to group, come to group,
> Chris and Maria come to group, We're singing about pizza today.

Activity 2

Children love to sing along with the book version of *The Lady with the Alligator Purse,* by Nadine Bernard Westcott.

Activity 3

Start by having the children clap the beats as they say the chant "Pizza" (activity 3.7). After several times through, substitute triangles for the claps. Children can tell what they like best on pizza.

Activity 4

Children can create patterns with cut-out shapes of pizza toppings. The children can chant the patterns. See the whole-math extension of activity 3.13 for examples of "pizza" patterns.

Activity 5

Divide the children into groups with each group providing a rhythm for this pizza ensemble (activity 3.13).

Activity 6

Change the field trip transition song (activity 7.14) to reflect an upcoming trip to the pizza parlor.

8.10 Babies

Sample Lesson Plan for Kindergartners

	Area	Activity	Why Selected
1.	song, whole-language extension	"Lullaby World" with big book	length and melody appropriate for kindergarten children can learn how to say baby and sleep in other languages
2.	rhythm	use baby rattles to play the rhythm of the word for *baby* in other languages	multicultural allows children to hear the rhythm of other languages
3.	literature	*Hush!* by Minfong Ho	excellent multicultural book from Thailand language is predictable and very rhythmic
4.	song, whole-language extension	"Hurry Mama" with class books	song encourages children to add their own words melody is easy to sing
5.	math (estimation)	children estimate number of pacifiers in a clear jar	coordinates with baby topic encourages numerical thinking
6.	song, whole-language extension	"Hush, Little Baby" with interactive chart	illustrates father's love for his baby children can follow the words on the chart as they sing can be used as a transition song

Description of Activities

Activity 1

Children can follow the words in the big book as they sing "Lullaby World" (activity 2.12). They are fascinated with how the words for *baby* and *sleep* look and sound in other languages.

Activity 2

Clap and chant the words for *baby* in other languages. Use baby rattles as maracas and substitute them for the claps.

Activity 3

Hush!, by Minfong Ho, shows a mother's love for her baby in rural Thailand. The book is predictable, and the language is very rhythmic.

Activity 4

For this lesson plan, it is assumed that children already know the song "Hurry Mama" (activity 2.9) well and have used it as a springboard for a writing activity. The children's pages are assembled into a class book. They can look at one another's words and pictures as they sing the song.

Activity 5

Children have seen babies with pacifiers and are excited to guess how many pacifiers are in the jar. Once they each have had a turn, they are eager to quantify the pacifiers and compare their guesses to the real amount.

Activity 6

Children can follow the words on the chart as they sing "Hush, Little Baby" (activity 2.13) together. Place each child's name on the chart and use it as a transition device.

8.11 Spring Weather

Sample Lesson Plan for Kindergartners

	Area	Activity	Why Selected
1.	song, whole-language extension	"Thunder" with big book	children are reassured by the words melody easy to sing children can follow the words in the big book as they sing
2.	literature	*It Looked Like Spilt Milk,* by Charles G. Shaw (big book)	predictable book coordinates with season and weather topic
3.	song	"Clouds" with flannelboard	good follow-up for *Spilt Milk* children can contribute their own ideas melody fits singing range of five year olds
4.	movement	children imitate cloud movements to music	encourages creative interpretation
5.	instruments, rhythm	"Thunder" ensemble	children can perform separate lines of music and hear them as a whole helps children focus on rhythmic patterns
6.	transition song	"Rain, Rain, Go Away"	children's names can be added to the song helps children move to the next activity

Description of Activities

Activity 1

Many children are afraid of thunder and storms, and the song "Thunder" (activity 2.10) reassures them. Children can follow the words in the big book as they sing the song.

Activity 2

It Looked Like Spilt Milk, by Charles G. Shaw, is predictable and is a kind of guessing game. It coordinates well with discussions of weather and clouds.

Activity 3

"Clouds" (activity 2.8) is a good follow-up for *It Looked Like Spilt Milk.* Teachers can add shapes from the book to the flannelboard and sing those words in the song. Children can suggest cloud shapes to add to the song.

Activity 4

Soft music provides a backdrop for children to interpret the movements of clouds with their bodies. The recording *Make Believe in Movement,* by Maya Doray, has a narrated section on cloud dramatization.

Activity 5

For this activity, add layers of melodic patterns to the "Thunder" song from earlier in the group time.

Activity 6

Add children's names to the familiar song "Rain, Rain, Go Away" to help them transition out of group. For example:

> Rain, rain, go away,
> Come again some other day,
> Angki and Sarah want to play.

8.12 Sea

Sample Lesson Plan for Kindergartners

	Area	Activity	Why Selected
1.	transition song	"Look at What We're Wearing" adaptation	focuses on clothing changes for seasons each child can be added to the song
2.	literature	*Blue Sea* by Robert Kalan (big book)	predictable book children can follow words and read along
3.	song, instruments, rhythm	"Swish, Swish, Swish" with water maracas	coordinates with *Blue Sea* water maracas create tone painting
4.	movement, musical concept (tempo)	"Turtle"	encourages creative movement slow movements help children focus on slow tempo coordinates with curriculum
5.	rhythm, math	shell patterns	rhythmic chanting of mathematical pattern helps children perceive them
6.	rhythm, instruments	"Rain, Rain, Go Away" ensemble	children can perform separate patterns and hear them as a whole helps children focus on rhythmic patterns
7.	transition song, whole-language extension	"If Your Name Begins"	focuses on initial letter of each child's name encourages comparison of written names

Description of Activities

Activity 1

Alter the song "Look at What We're Wearing" (activity 7.11) to say, "Now that it's warm outside." Add each child's name and clothing to the song.

Activity 2

Children delight in the book *Blue Sea,* by Robert Kalan. They soon read along with the big book.

Activity 3

"Swish, Swish, Swish" (activity 2.15) coordinates with *Blue Sea*. Children can accompany the song with water maracas.

Activity 4

Children can recite the turtle poem along with the teacher (activity 4.7). Then, as the teacher again recites the poem, they can act out the movements of the turtle, snail, and crab.

Activity 5

Create patterns with seashells for children to chant and clap. Children can also suggest patterns. Chanting and clapping the patterns helps some children perceive them.

Activity 6

The "Rain, Rain, Go Away" ensemble (activity 4.13) involves three children playing different melodic patterns while the rest of the class sings. It gives children the opportunity to perform and hear individual lines combining to form a complete piece of music.

Activity 7

In the song "If Your Name Begins" (activity 7.13), children have to figure out whose name starts with the letter you sing. This song helps children focus on the initial letter and compare the way names look and sound.

Resource Information

The following list contains information on the books and recordings mentioned in *More Than Singing* that may be useful when trying to locate these resources at libraries or stores.

Chapter Two:

A Is for Aloha, by Stephanie Feeney (Honolulu: UP of Hawaii, 1980).
Barnyard Banter, by Denise Fleming (New York: Holt, 1994).
Bat Time, by Ruth Horowitz (Washington, D.C.: Four Winds, 1991).
Before I Was Born, by Harriet Ziefert (New York: Knopf, 1989).
The Big Fat Worm, by Nancy Van Laan (New York: Knopf, 1987).
Bird, by Moira Butterfield (New York: Simon & Schuster, 1991).
Blue Sea, by Robert Kalan (New York: Greenwillow Books, 1979).
Chicka, Chicka, Boom Boom, by Bill Martin Jr. and John Archambault (New York: Simon & Schuster, 1989).
The Cloud Book, by Tomie de Paola (New York: Scholastic, 1975).
The Cuddlers, by Stacy Towle Morgan (Schaumburg, IL: La Leche League, 1993).
Flap Your Wings and Try, by Charlotte Pomerantz (New York: Greenwillow, 1989).
Footprints in the Snow, by Cynthia Benjamin (New York: Scholastic, 1994).
Goodnight Owl, by Pat Hutchins (New York: Macmillan, 1972).
Humbug Witch, by Lorna Balian (Nashville: Abingdon, 1987).
Hurricane, by David Wiesner (New York: Clarion, 1990).
Hush!, by Minfong Ho (New York: Orchard Books, 1996).
Hush, Little Baby, by Aliki (New York: Simon & Schuster, 1968).
I Can Be a Firefighter, by Rebecca Hankin (Danbury, CT: Childrens Press, 1985).
I Love My Daddy Because . . . , by Laurel Porter-Gaylord (New York: Dutton, 1991).
I Love My Mommy Because . . . , by Laurel Porter-Gaylord (New York: Dutton, 1991).
I'm Going To Be a Firefighter, by Edith Kunhardt (New York: Scholastic, 1989).
In the Snow, by Huy Voun Lee (New York: Holt, 1995).
It Looked Like Spilt Milk, by Charles G. Shaw (New York: Harper, 1947).
K Is for Kiss Goodnight, by Jill Sardegna (New York: Bantam, 1994).
Max the Music-Maker, by Miriam B. Stechler and Alice S. Kandell (New York: Lothrop, 1980).
More More More, Said the Baby, by Vera B. Williams (New York: Greenwillow, 1990).
The Napping House, by Audrey Wood (New York: Harcourt, 1984).
Navajo ABC, by Luci Tapahonso and Eleanor Schick (New York: Simon & Schuster, 1995).
Nuts to You!, by Lois Ehlert (New York: Harcourt, 1993).

Peter's Chair, by Ezra Jack Keats (New York: Harper, 1967).
A Pocket for Corduroy, by Don Freeman (New York: Viking, 1978).
Rain (Lynnfield, MA: Wonder Books, 1972).
Rat-a-Tat, Pitter Pat, by Alan Benjamin (New York: Crowell, 1987).
The Real-Skin Rubber Monster Mask, by Mirian Cohen (New York: Greenwillow, 1990).
Red Leaf, Yellow Leaf, by Lois Ehlert (New York: Harcourt, 1991).
Sleep, Sleep, Sleep, by Nancy Van Laan (Boston: Little Brown, 1995).
Snow on Snow on Snow, by Cheryl Chapman (New York: Dial, 1994).
The Snowy Day, by Ezra Jack Keats (New York: Viking, 1962).
Something Queer on Vacation, by Elizabeth Levy (New York: Delacorte, 1980).
Stellaluna, by Janell Cannon (New York: Harcourt, 1993).
Swimmy, by Leo Lionni (New York: Knopf, 1963).
Too Much Noise, by Ann McGovern (Boston: Houghton, 1967).
Tough Boris, by Mem Fox (New York: Harcourt, 1994).
Umbrella, Taro Yashima (New York: Viking, 1958).
Welcoming Babies, by Margy Burns Knight (Gardiner, ME: Tilbury House, 1994).
When the Teddy Bears Came, by Martin Waddell (Cambridge, MA: Candlewick, 1995).
The Wind Blew, by Pat Hutchins (New York: Macmillan, 1974).
The World Sings Goodnight (Silver Wave Records, SC803).

Chapter Three:

Aunt Flossie's Hats, by Elizabeth Fitzgerald Howard (New York: Clarion, 1991).
The Black Snowman, by Phil Mendez (New York: Scholastic, 1989).
Caps for Sale, by Esphyr Slobodkina (Reading, MA: Addison-Wesley, 1968).
The Carrot Seed, by Ruth Krauss (New York: Harper, 1945).
Corduroy, by Don Freeman (New York: Viking, 1968).
Curious George, by Margret and H. A. Rey (Boston: Houghton Mifflin, 1966).
Digging Up Dinosaurs, by Aliki (New York: Crowell, 1988).
Dinosaur, Dinosaur, by Byron Barton (New York: Crowell, 1989).
Eating the Alphabet, by Lois Ehlert(New York: Harcourt, 1989).
Flower Garden, by Eve Bunting (New York: Harcourt, 1994).
Golden Bear, by Ruth Young (New York: Viking, 1992).
Growing Vegetable Soup, by Lois Ehlert (New York: Harcourt, 1987).
Hats, Hats, Hats, by Ann Morris (New York: Lothrop, 1989).
I Went Walking, by Sue Williams (New York: Harcourt, 1989).
The Lady with the Alligator Purse, by Nadine Bernard Westcott (Boston: Little Brown, 1988).
A Letter to Amy, by Ezra Jack Keats (New York: Harper, 1968).
The Lotus Seed, by Sherry Garland (New York: Harcourt, 1993).
Me Too, by Susan Winter (New York: Dorling Kindersley, 1993).
My Best Friend, by Pat Hutchins (New York: Greenwillow, 1993).
My Friends, by Taro Gomi (San Francisco: Chronicle, 1990).
The Napping House, by Audrey Wood (New York: Harcourt, 1984).
Pizza Party, by Grace Maccarone (New York: Scholastic, 1994).
A Pocket for Corduroy, by Don Freeman (New York: Viking, 1978).
Pumpkin Pumpkin, by Jeanne Titherington (New York: Greenwillow, 1986).
The Quilt, by Ann Jonas (New York: Greenwillow, 1984).
Rain, by Peter Spier (New York: Doubleday, 1982).
Rosie's Walk, by Pat Hutchins (New York: Macmillan, 1968).
Silly Sally, by Audrey Wood (New York: Harcourt, 1992).
The Snowy Day, by Ezra Jack Keats (New York: Viking, 1962).
Tickle Tickle, by Helen Oxenbury (New York: Aladdin, 1987).
Tyrannosaurus Was a Beast, by Jack Prelutsky (New York: Greenwillow, 1988).

Umbrella, by Taro Yashima (New York: Viking, 1958).
What Is Your Language, by Debra Leventhal (New York: Dutton, 1994).
Where Can It Be? by Ann Jonas (New York: Greenwillow, 1986).

Chapter Five:

Changes, by R. Carlos Nakai (Canyon Records, CR-615).

Chapter Six:

Africa: Drum, Chant and Instrumental Music (Electra/Asylum/Nonesuch Records, 9 72073-4).
All Fall Down, by Helen Oxenbury (New York: Aladdin, 1987).
Andy, An Alaskan Tale, by Susan Welsh-Smith (New York: Cambridge UP, 1988).
A Children's Zoo, by Tana Hoban (New York: Greenwillow, 1985).
Clap Hands, by Helen Oxenbury (New York: Aladdin, 1987).
Color Dance, by Ann Jonas (New York: Greenwillow, 1989).
Dance at Grandpa's, by Laura Ingalls Wilder (New York: Scholastic, 1994).
Dancing with the Indians, by Angela Shelf Medearis (New York: Holiday House, 1991).
Dear Zoo, by Rod Campbell (Washington, D.C.: Four Winds, 1982).
Freight Train, by Donald Crews (New York: Mulberry, 1978).
Homrong, by the National Dance Company of Cambodia (Realworld Records, 7567-91734-4).
In the Snow, by Huy Voun Lee (New York: Holt, 1995).
Lili on Stage, by Rachel Isadora (New York: Putnam, 1995).
Lion Dancer, by Kate Waters and Madeline Sloveny-Low (New York: Scholastic, 1990).
Little Blue and Little Yellow, by Leo Lionni (New York: Scholastic, 1993).
Mimi's Tutu, by Tynia Thomassie (New York: Scholastic, 1996).
The Mitten, by Jan Brett (New York: Putnam, 1989).
More than Counting, by Sally Moomaw and Brenda Hieronymus (St. Paul: Redleaf, 1995).
Mouse Paint, by Ellen Stoll Walsh (New York: Harcourt, 1989).
My Ballet Class, by Rachel Isadora (New York: Greenwillow, 1980).
Nuts to You!, by Lois Ehlert (New York: Harcourt, 1993).
Powwow, by George Ancona (New York: Harcourt, 1993).
Raffi Songs to Read (New York: Crown, 1989).
Red Dancing Shoes, by Denise Lewis Patrick (New York: Tambourine, 1993).
Silent Lotus, by Jeanne M. Lee (New York: Farrar, 1991).
Smilin' Island of Song, by Cedella Marley Booker (Music for Little People, 9 42521-4).
Song and Dance Man, by Karen Ackerman (New York: Knopf, 1988).
Tickle Tickle, by Helen Oxenbury (New York: Aladdin, 1987).
The Train Ride, by June Crebbin (Cambridge, MA: Candlewick, 1995).
Trains, by Byron Barton (New York: Harper, 1986).
Two Tiny Mice, by Alan Baker (New York: Scholastic, 1990).
The Very Hungry Caterpillar, by Eric Carle (New York: Philomel, 1969).
What Happens at the Zoo, by Judith E. Rinard (Washington, D.C.: National Geographic, 1984).

Chapter 7:

Africa: Drum, Chant and Instrumental Music (Electra/Asylum/Nonesuch Records, 9 72073-4).
D is for Dulcimer, by Glenn Morgan (Fishbite Recordings, 9001-4).
Dream Catcher, by Kevin Locke (EarthBeat! Recordings, EB 2696).

Drums & Voices of Korea, by Samul-Nori (Electra/Asylum/Nonesuch Records, 9 72093-4).

Homrong, by Musicians of the National Dance Company of Cambodia (Realworld Records, 7567-91734-4).

How the West Was Lost, by Peter Kater with R. Carlos Nakai (Silver Wave Records, SC 801).

Japan: Traditional Vocal & Instrumental Music, by Ensemble Nipponia (Electra/Asylum/Nonesuch Records, 9 72072-4).

The Oud, by H. Aram Gulezyan (Lyrichord Recordings, LLCT 7160).

Quinchuquimanda: Music of the Andes, by Karullacta (contact C. Quinche, 612-789-1392).

Smilin' Island of Song, by Cedella Marley Booker (Music for Little People, 9 42521-4).

United States International Powwow (Makoché Music/BMI, MC 0123).

The World Sings Goodnight (Silver Wave Records, SC 803).

Chapter 8:

Caps for Sale, by Esphyr Slobodkina (Reading, MA: Addison-Wesley, 1968).

Color Dance, by Ann Jonas (New York: Greenwillow, 1989).

Blue Sea, by Robert Kalan (New York: Greenwillow, 1979).

Hush!, by Minfong Ho (New York: Orchard, 1996).

It Looked Like Spilt Milk, by Charles G. Shaw (New York: Harper, 1992).

The Lady with the Alligator Purse, by Nadine Bernard Westcott (Boston: Little Brown, 1988).

Make Believe in Movement, by Maya Doray (Long Beach, NJ: Kimbo Educational, 1976).

My Friend, by Taro Gomi (San Francisco: Chronicle, 1990).

Index of Songs

Chants and Poems